Please Unlock the Door

Shara Waller

ISBN 979-8-89112-681-7 (Paperback)
ISBN 979-8-89309-133-5 (Hardcover)
ISBN 979-8-89112-682-4 (Digital)

Covenant Books
11661 Hwy 707
Murrells Inlet, SC 29576
www.covenantbooks.com

CONTENTS

CHAPTER 1

Secrets: All I Know Is

Our Father, who art in heaven, hallowed be thy name; thy kingdom come; thy will be done; on earth as it is in heaven. Give us this day our daily bread. And forgive us our trespasses, as we forgive those who trespass against us. And lead us not into temptation, but deliver us from evil. For thine is the kingdom, the power, and the glory forever (Matthew 6:9b–13 KJV). Amen!

> The LORD *is* my shepherd; I shall not want. He maketh me to lie down in green pastures: He leadeth me beside the still waters. He restoreth my soul: He leadeth me in the paths of righteousness for his name's sake. Yea, though I walk through the valley of the shadow of death, I will fear no evil: for thou *art* with me; Thy rod and thy staff they comfort me. Thou preparest a table before me in the presence of mine enemies: Thou anointest my head with oil; my cup runneth over. Surely goodness and mercy shall follow me all the days of my life: And I will dwell in the house of the LORD for ever. (Psalm 23 KJV)

You see, there was a time when I knew for sure I was locked in, but I really wasn't. In the beginning, that's what I thought, you know. Children, especially one like me—an only child, spoiled rotten (which I didn't know at the time)—believed they were running the show. I thought I knew everything. No, I knew I did.

To understand me and my marvels, one must grasp how little Miss Brilliant came about. I want to let you in slowly; just crack the door a bit. I can't fully open up all the way yet, you see, with me in charge of myself and how I am. Okay, this almost first grader will open the door a bit more so you won't be in the dark because the light (John 8:12) needs to be on. There's no need to fear. Secrets are going to come out. Just remember that the beginning of the journey is from the perspective of a know-it-all superior first grader. So far, I'm sure you're saying that this little Miss Brilliant has it all figured out early in life—just about.

I was born on May 25, 1955, to a single mother nicknamed Cookie. That's what they told me. The reason I say that is that, as an adult, I was at a doctor's office where they had an error in the patient's chart on my birthday. The office worker asked me if I was sure, so I told her no, not really; that's what my mom and family members told me. How does anyone (a baby) know when they're actually born? I don't know anything about the day of my birth, so all I could do was go by what they said. She looked at me as if I was crazy and needed to be in an asylum, which, later on, may be true, because you'll see. The charity hospital where I was born did goof up the correct spelling of my first name, which I found out almost eighteen years later. That's another story, but for now, it's about me entering this world with obstacles already in my way.

Cookie gave birth to me with her two sisters around. Cookie's mother (Momoa) was at another hospital with my grandfather, who died the day I was born. I really do believe this was a state asylum. All I knew was that he was sick and where we lived. The only hospital around was where I was born. People drove miles to get there, so why was he somewhere else? I, myself, was born with a blue veil (back then, that's what they called it) over my face and a pinhole near the ear. Your guess is as good as mine, but this covering, so I was told, was a premonition—so maybe it explains a lot of what I know beforehand, but I wish it had foretold more of my future. It didn't, but yet and still, I was brilliant.

Remember, the best-kept secrets are never told—a Momoa quote. You should be ready to read. Now the first time the light came on was in my first chapter: Secrets. Now we were on to secrets, or that's what it seemed like to me.

I had just come home from school. I was a first grader, five going on six, but it wasn't summertime yet because school was out in May, after my birthday. Oh, and by the way, I was a brilliant first grader, if I must say so myself. We received a phone call from my aunt to speak to my grandmother, a.k.a. Momoa, but she hadn't come home from work yet. As soon as she got home, she needed to call her sister's house, a.k.a. my great-aunt, since she had no phone back then. She said it was an emergency, and I told her I would tell Momoa.

My house consisted of another aunt and uncle, Momoa, Cookie, my mama, and my aunt's son. He was there for me when I came home every day. I told him about the call, just in case this brilliant scholar would forget because, you know, once we start playing outside, I'd get so caught up in the fun and games that everything else would just slip my mind. Well, Momoa got home. She was a cook at a restaurant and, by the way, the best in the *world*, something I knew myself. I was on the carport playing, so I told her myself about what my aunt said. Momoa usually always had something for me, and being as nosy as I was, I went inside with her. Remember, little Miss Brilliant was a first grader, and what I heard was somebody was being taken to the hospital, or something like that. I knew by the look on Momoa's face she was upset. Fear, as I know it today, was what I saw. Tears soon flowed, and by then, panic was in me because this couldn't be good. I had never, ever seen Momoa cry that I could remember. I asked her who was sick, and she said her mama. *What?*

Now we're on to secrets!

How could my grandmother have a mama? I thought the world began with her for my family. You thought she seemed upset? Trust me, I think that was my first traumatic experience. Oh my god, awe, disbelief, and devastation, just to name a few, set in. That ain't so started in little Miss Brilliant. Now you already know I was spoiled to the hilt, very much like today. Most of those who are only child go down that path. I don't ever remember my grandmother crying, but if I could've had a conniption fit, trust me, I would have, but I was not that spoiled to try that at this time. So now my world meant, in all honesty, that Momoa had loved someone more than me. I know you're saying little Miss Brilliant must be insane. Momoa had seven children of her own, so how in the world could I have come to that conclusion? Well, I did. I was only five going on six. You see, now I live in my own world and am used to being all and knowing all. You'll see why sanity or insanity came into play in my life. I came to the conclusion quickly, and whoever this person was, the *war was on*!

Insanity came a little too fast. Can you believe I already knew this rival? My aunt, who lived in the country, took care of this old lady whom everybody called Big Mama, including me because everybody else did. My aunt's family helped with all the chores for her: cleaning, cooking, bathing, I mean everything. I really didn't do much but be in the way. I had no idea this old lady, whom we called Big Mama, was my great-grandmother. I had already made up my mind that whoever she was, I didn't like her trying to come and take my grandmother's love. She made Momoa cry too, and I wasn't having or feeling it. Before I knew who she was, during a visit, I asked to try that snuff thing. My cousins were doing it, so I should too. How hard could it be?

I saw her dip snuff, and one of my cousins was doing it too, so I asked Big Mama if I could have some. She put it in my lower lip, and it started burning right away. I didn't think about the spit, not paying attention to what she did. Every now and then, she and my cousin were putting something up to their mouth. She had on a big apron with pockets; now I know that she was putting that in that little napkin with that little cup inside. Little Miss Brilliant, after all, had plenty of book smarts, but the common sense, the real deal, hadn't kicked in yet. When I asked her what to do with the juice, she said, "Swallow it." Sure enough, I did. That was my last visit to the country. I remember I was sick as a dog. I remember the world spinning; the next thing I remember was a car ride to the hospital in the city. My cousins dipped, and Big Mama too; they didn't get sick. I couldn't understand that. No one told me not to swallow. I guess, as they say, that's what you get for begging. Sane or insane? I told my mama, Cookie, and grandmother Momoa what had happened; they were upset. The excuse was she was an old lady and didn't know any better. Little Miss Brilliant couldn't believe this lady made me sick. She was dangerous.

When I came home from the hospital, I had cake, balloons, and a few friends over, some presents, like a birthday party. So you see how little Miss Brilliant's life was like. About a week after I got out of the hospital, I noticed the house was being rearranged for Momoa's mother. I had no idea. I couldn't wait to see her because I was going to show her what I was working with, or so I thought. This was the lady the phone call was about. Oh yeah, this was on. I got out of school, and an ambulance pulled up at our house. I really believe this was my first time seeing or being close to one, and to be honest, I was scared of it. We didn't own a car when I was little, but this thing here was overwhelming, yet and still, I didn't care who was getting out. Why didn't I get a ride in an ambulance? I was sick too. How much trauma can a first grader take? I really think this was the first time if I had a can of whoop-ass, I would have pulled it out. That ambulance topped all my cake, presents, and balloons; they didn't compare. You see how little Miss Brilliant thinks.

Lo and behold, this hospital bed was being pulled out with this four-foot-eleven-inch woman we call Big Mama on it, looking like the old lady from the country, with her moaning and groaning. It was another trauma to my very being. I really believe that was the first time I said, "Lord, have mercy."

CHAPTER 2

Arrival of the Ambulance Murderess

She came in and took over at my house—mind you, my house. With a dose of reality, the more I looked at Big Mama, she was a replica of Cookie, my mama. Now we were about to arrive at this insanity thing. Her height and stature were more a ten-foot-tall woman in the room, but she was only four feet eleven inches tall. What's going on here? She sucked up all the air. You would think Big Mama was her mother. Cookie was slowly and truly slipping into that world. I had always known Cookie was somewhere else 90 percent of the time, but she was doing her best; no one had to tell me that. I loved her fearlessly. I was not sure what was wrong, but I knew something was. No one knows the future, but I did know that this new beginning with Big Mama wasn't going to be a good thing.

Sanity is a strong word, but it wasn't happening at my house, and I do mean my house, not hers. This person, from day one, took over completely. I wanted to leave home, run away, disappear, hide, or just take a rocket to the moon and not come back. That should be far enough.

I knew the country life wasn't for me with my two-pound self, but this was my only choice. I'm the person who always thinks I can do better; well, that was how little Miss Brilliant thinks. "Monkey see, monkey do" was my motto. Trying to do what I saw my cousins do—if they could, I should be able to also. We'd draw the water to take a bath and heat it on the fire outside. There was no electricity, so you know there's no TV, music, or refrigerator, but the woodstove cooked like our stove, even better than the modern stove at your home, but that was about all. Trying out the rub board on my vacay tore my knuckles up. The only thing I was good at was shooing the chickens to get eggs, and to be honest, I was kind of scared of them too. I saw my aunt wring a chicken's neck; it took off and was still running. I can laugh now, but at that time, nooo! I wasn't laughing, chuckling, or anything of the sort. Trust me, I had made up my mind this was my last country vacay.

Before Big Mama tried to kill me, my uncle shot and killed a donkey, mule, burro, or whatever you call them. I called him Baby because he was a baby whatever. He had been plowing the field every day, working Baby to the bone from sunup till sundown, so one day Baby couldn't take it no more. He just knelt down and wouldn't and couldn't get up. I was sitting on the back steps, and I heard him say, "You just sit right there till I get back." Baby couldn't move to save his life; he was worn out. Another trauma was when my uncle came back with the shotgun and shot Baby in the head. Trust me, I saw Westerns on TV, but this, oh no! My aunt said, "You've done it," so now what would make me want to run away from home to here?

You can tell at this stage I needed a plan.

CHAPTER 3

The Plan Didn't Work or Did It?

You, this first grader saw lots of things, but the real, real was the more I looked, the less I liked what I saw. Some things you don't look for but just see, and I did, very early in life, but I had to figure these things out right then. The insanity did seep in and go through.

When Big Mama really got settled in, she wanted to be Cookie's baby. I didn't get a break. You know I was having or feeling that way because, by the way, Cookie was mine just like Momoa, and I was not jealous. Every day when I'd get home, Big Mama wanted to know what I did: read a story, this, that, and the other, so being as brilliant as I was, I was going to fix this.

I couldn't come home and play for a little while before Momoa came home, and I knew she had a snack from her job. When Cookie got home, playtime was *over*.

The remedy for Big Mama was that I couldn't read. I was too little, and I was only six years old by this time. Well, don't say or even think about it. You know I was still little. So Big Mama told Cookie, and she went off. It didn't take much; her demeanor was a quiet person. No, I didn't get that trait. Her feelings were easily hurt, and me? I'd give it back to you like a flamethrower. Cookie ranted and raved all evening. When my uncle came home and asked what was happening—and of course, I was his favorite niece in probably a headcount of thirty girls; seriously, but you know, no one is like me—he didn't say much, but he knew Big Mama; after all, she was his grandmother, not mine.

So on day 2 of this reading ritual, I got even smarter, or so I thought. I read the first few pages and then the back and then said, "The End." I had been at school all day and was tired. I'd had a hard day. I was only six, and by the way, did I tell you I was in the gifted group? Yep, but at this stage, I wasn't gifted enough. Cookie came home, and Big Mama told her I did not read to her; I was just "calling words." Well, I found out, so little Miss Brilliant said, "If I read the story, why do I need to explain it?" If you can't explain what you're reading to someone else, you're just "calling words." So there you have it; Big Mama struck again.

My mother really loved her Big Mama and would handle her like a baby, and she ate it up, spoon, bowl, what's in the bowl, and what's outside the bowl. Yeah, I know what you are saying, no, I wasn't jealous because I was closer to Momoa. Big Mama could do no wrong in Cookie's eyes, even when she was telling stories about me. My school days were not over even when I got home. Cookie's new baby got all the attention. Look, she was already on my list in my head to seek revenge for how she did Momoa, which at the time was the only one on the list that I could think of. This new trick really brought out the insane side of my mother. It took my uncle and cousins to get some order in the house. Cookie was really a sweet, quiet person most of the time, but not today. I didn't know my dad really broke her too. May the Lord have mercy when I do find out. Father moved down the road; I was going to need some mercy. My uncle didn't take my side of what I did, but I do remember him saying, "The child needs a break." As to why he was home early, I don't know but thank God, He sent him home to spare the rod that day. Big Mama looked mad. She didn't get the last laugh that day, but neither did I because Cookie was really unhappy with me, and my uncle too. What was a first grader to do?

Can you believe that was when I learned to really enjoy reading? Every day, I could hardly wait to get home after school, get undressed, and get in bed with Big Mama. Yeah, Big Mama and I got close until Christmas. The family bought me a color TV. Yes, sir. That was in the sixties when they first came out, and you know I had to have one. Big Mama was wheeled in, and we were all watching a

Christmas show. Some neighbors were there too until they got their own. I didn't really mind because if they had kids, I had someone to play with, and Cookie wouldn't be worrying about me because I was at home. Thank You, Jesus. Christmas Eve came, and we were watching a Christmas special. Big Mama had on her little apron as usual. Big Mama had a lesson to teach, especially when asking for something. She always had some kind of treat in hand. You know, I was all about that quick lesson: if you ask someone for something, be sure to specify what you want. I asked her for a piece of orange. Now let me give credit where credit is due; she peeled it for me and gave me a slice. I didn't say a piece, I said a slice. And she threw the rest away. That's what I asked for in her eyes, so the next time, believe me, I asked for the whole thing.

As we were watching the Christmas special, Big Mama thought the lady on the screen was watching and making fun of her. You have to remember, in the country, there was no electricity and no running water. She'd never seen a TV. She was looking rather odd at this, too, because we were all laughing while cracking pecans for me and her. I said *me* and *her*, that's right. I told you we got close. All of a sudden, Big Mama rolled the chair herself, so you see, she wasn't as helpless as she made it seem. Rolling over to that beautiful new TV (when I think on it, it was as pretty as that big piano I died for, took six weeks of lessons, and decided I didn't like it) with that little hammer, and it was a cute little hammer. I could handle it by myself if need be. She rolled over (crack) and hit that screen. She said, "Now she'll quit looking at me," and yelled, "Will y'all quit laughing?" Big Mama cried for real for the first time. Can you believe Cookie was her comforter, but this time I was the one to console her? It broke my heart to see real tears, and that was when I realized I loved her. She didn't know any better, and everything was new, even the house, phone, radio, TV, and all the strange people she didn't know. How could I do her that way? Yeah, I got bent about the TV, but after all, she didn't understand. Of course, I got another one, but now I've got a baby sister, and she was just older, so I was not sharing her. Move over, Cookie.

It wasn't long before she died. They had to keep amputating this, that, and the other. It took a while for me to get over that, but I still got in her bed every afternoon, except on weekends, continuing my journey of learning and going places in those books. Who knows, those places are real, and Big Mama took me there. Sometimes, we would just be riding on a buckboard in the country, in her mind, and I could see it too, past my aunt's house in the country. It was just me and Big Mama. There were plenty of days the whiff would sneak up, but I thought at that time it would be just the scent of older people, but it's not, at least not in my case. I knew better than that, but it didn't matter 'cause I love me some Big Mama. In the end, it was no longer a secret. Now I know who she is, like everybody else. So you see, secrets get out.

I'll be seeing you in my travels—Egypt, Italy, but, most of all, heaven. Love you, Big Mama!

CHAPTER 4

A Dad—Where Is Mine?

Little Miss Brilliant didn't have one. The genius was not aware even though all my little girlfriends had one. I wasn't even aware of people being married. I know, I know, I was just as dense on some things. Remember, I was about five to six years old, and I never wondered about it. After all, I had an uncle, Cookie's baby brother, who did what their father should do. Well, the question came up by one of my friends. There were six of us, and their dads treated me like I was a daughter to them and, by the way, their moms and dads were all—what I now call—professional people: nurses, teachers, railroad men, police officers, and a principal. One day, one of my friend's dad got hurt in an auto accident. This accident was not something I really knew about, but little Miss Brilliant, being nosy, heard the rumors, and it wasn't nice because I didn't know much about what I heard. Too young to get it, but I knew when I grew up, I was going to marry him. He was the only one who would give me a ride on his high-tech chair. Big Mama had one too, but you had to push hers. So you know I had to find out who this dad was, what his name was, and where he was.

I couldn't believe another secret had come to the surface, and I didn't know why nobody told me. It was coming, but I wasn't going to like it. In the second grade, I found out who, what, and where he was, but finding out why he was not here was heartbreaking. The first thing that I was told he ever sent me was a bad leather-strap Mickey Mouse watch. It was red in color, and no one else had one like it. Yeah, my little gal pals got one after me, but I had it first!

We had to show and tell at school after Christmas, and I proudly took that watch, and let me tell you, I had the floor. I should have won the prize, but you know, it was always someone else who won. This boy got a gerbil rat; we girls were all screaming and yelling (another trauma). I had never seen anything like that. He won because we had more boys in the class; not one girl voted for that thing. How could that gerbil rat win over my bad, by the way, huge-face moving pieces that worked on the inside were made of shiny patent leather. Mickey's hands had big gloves on them, and they did everything but talk, and you know my show-and-tell was better. I must admit by the end of the day, I liked that gerbil. I wanted one for myself. I went home and asked Mom, but you know I know you know what happened.

I got over that answer quickly and fast. What I didn't get over was (don't snoop, I quit being nosy after this) the letter I found when I put the watch back in the jewelry box. This astute second grader loved reading. Big Mama taught me that, remember? This letter didn't have my name on it. Well, you know, that didn't mean a thing to me. My momma Cookie's name was on it, so that was my permission. She was my mother, and I should have every right to read it. You see how my mind works by now, well. Another war was on, by now since Big Mama (God rest her soul, and I really mean that), had died. The letter said a whole lot, but for sure what I understood was "I was a mistake." Yes, I knew what a mistake was. I was a second grader who was no longer calling words. I was in the accelerated class, and we were all a little brilliant.

I had never met or even seen the man, but it was on. After reading this letter, now came the actual meeting on my first trip to California, which was where he had been since I was nine months old.

I remember our next-door neighbor had a baby. She already had about seven or eight kids. I played with them a lot. Her oldest daughter would do my hair sometimes, and she was beautiful to me and always nice. When that new baby came along, I was really interested because I don't think I had ever seen one. I really liked her too. You know how I wanted that gerbil? Well, I wanted that baby too. I asked

Mama how they got that baby. I was told from the cabbage patch. Well, my aunt, you remember, had Big Mama in the country before she came to us, and rows and rows of cabbages. Well, the next time I went down there, I would look for a little sister like the neighbor had. I never saw one. This little brilliant girl was in the seventh grade when I found out there was no Santa Claus, another secret I didn't know. Can you believe I got up in front of my class full of overachievers and said what Santa brought me for Christmas? You talk about being the laughingstock of America. What! You see, something was wrong with this picture.

I can't say I had a sheltered life, but the second-grade summer trip to meet the missing dad really started everything. To make it easy, the trip turned out to be a battle of returning me home. I did meet my family on my father's side since I had another grandmother and grandfather, aunts, uncles, cousins, and just a whole other world I never knew I was missing. How could I when I didn't know about them? My world was everybody that was in it. Well, I met and fell in love with his mom and baby sister whom I look like, and finally, seeing him, I realized she looked like him, so there have it.

The return got really ugly. That family had money, whereas my family did not, but I never suffered for anything. Violin, cello, piano—anything little Miss Brilliant wanted. Toys galore, a huge bike that I had too, as I grew into my own stereo, color TV, anything made on earth. I'll admit I had it, but I had to earn it. Good grades were mandatory, as was obedience. I remember one *C* on a report card. Mama said I better not ever come home with that, especially since it was in conduct. The teacher explained she gave me that grade, and my little gal pals, not because we were bad, but because the rest of the class got *F*s for not remaining quiet when she left the room. Since we did obey, she gave us the *C*. Do you think Mama was hearing that? She said it in front of me, Momoa, and my uncle, stating, "She has one *C* in her name and that's the only one that I accept." Well, trust me, that was the only time a *C* ever appeared in my whole life. Cookie wasn't playing!

Remember me being a mistake? Child support was the issue of my being returned. It was not about love or wanting me. I was returned with a hell of a fight, but can you believe that letter did the trick? From time to time, I still visited my grandparents at their home in my hometown. You see, back then they could afford to live there, and I got to really know them, until…

I had other little cousins who visited from all over during summer break. I liked them too, but I was the only one whose parents were not married. So you see how much I have grown. One of their neighbors asked who I was, noting I looked just like my dad's mom. I really am a carbon copy of her, my dad, and his baby sister. My grandfather said I was so-and-so's bastard. He treated me differently than the other light-skinned grandkids who were his coloring, but my grandmother would treat me so special because she'd always say, "You're mine."

It's funny how memories can be hurtful. I was a third grader, but I did know if he was short on apples, orange candy, or really anything. I was the one who was left behind, but my grandmother would truly outdo him by a mile so I wouldn't feel bad, but deep down inside, I did. You know, I called Momoa, my mom's mom (remember), to ask about that *bastard* word. She asked where I got that from, and I told her. I was a teenager when I found out. I want you to know my mom's sister turned the corner on two wheels in her four-wheel car; she lived not far away and picked me up with my Momoa. I don't think Momoa had ever gotten in someone's face, but that day, as they say now, "she was off the chain." She grabbed me up off that porch, and she didn't even get my clothes, luggage, books, or anything, not even shoes that were lying on the porch. She told grandpa a few words; they were new to me. Not sure she didn't invent a few, but that was another summer vacation gone, and I thought Mama Cookie could go off.

Cookie was really in a faraway place by now. One day after school, I had come home, and she wore me out with her belt. Now what I had done? Why? To this day I can only say she had a nervous breakdown. She had gotten to the point where she couldn't hold a cup or glass without everything spilling out. You see, she had worried herself to the bone. I don't remember her not having two jobs at a time. No, Mom wasn't like my girl pals' moms. She wasn't a professional, but here was what she did: maid at the school during the day and worked evenings at a hospital. I remember once she came home crying because a patient threw a bowel movement on her.

Let me tell you, Cookie went to work all starched up, clean as a whistle. She really looked like a nurse, like one of my girl pals' moms. I always thought this actress was a replica of my mom with her exotic voice and features back in the day. Her tears really hurt me because she seemed like she was my age. Momoa had to really comfort her, like she did me when all wasn't right in the world. I was paying attention, not quite understanding what was really going on here. I think for once in my life I wasn't jealous of Momoa loving my mom because she needed it, and after all, Cookie was her baby.

In less than a week, Cookie had to be put away in an asylum for a while, a long while. Momoa told me someone had given her LSD. I know a little about drugs, but this trip she was on lasted the rest of her life and mine. This was when psychiatric visits started and continued for thirty years. After her first stay there, when she came home, she was more quiet. Today, I call it melancholy. She still chain-smoked two cigarettes at a time, lit before the other one was out, and she even went back to work. Not two jobs at a time, but as an elevator girl in a big-name department store during the daytime. On the weekend, the movies, anything playing at the show, new, I saw it. It was all day long, but my girlfriends and I loved it. I see now I never went alone, but at the time, I didn't notice.

Pretty soon, Cookie got tired of that and other things at home, so she thought she could do better in California. She was the only one of her siblings who had a high school education, so I guess that was her incentive. But I do believe my dad was still in her heart. I didn't see him or any of his family while we were there. She let me finish my first year of junior high. I guess the passing of my uncle, who was two years older than her, mattered. In fact, it was the same year, the same day a famous politician was slain. My uncle made sure I was dressed while she went to work and walked me to elementary school every day. He couldn't read or write, but he was a math genius, and I do mean that. He could do any kind of math in his head, no paper and pencil, just up top. Now you know I was little Miss Brilliant! In the second grade, I remember we had to learn all the multiplication tables (from 1 to 12). The teacher said that on a Monday and wanted us to be ready on Wednesday. What? She normally started everything in alphabetical order, so it would be a while before she got to the *J*'s, or so I thought. I went home and told my uncle about it.

"Come on, I'm smart but…"

He said, "Let's get started. No niece of mine is a dumb bunny."

It's funny, the things you can remember from childhood that stick with you.

I was starting to have some trouble, but hey, I've got a while. She's going to do the *L* last name first. So itchy to be in a hurry. Don't you know he made me dance my way from 1 to 12 for two nights? He said, "You like dancing so much," so I remember a song about baby workouts and that was what I did. I must have done the shake, swim, twist, slide, skate, monkey shake, and jerk until I thought I was still jerking into a spasm. Lo and behold, on Wednesday morning, I was called first. My teacher called two other teachers to watch this show.

I was an office helper at an elementary school on the intercom about late buses, attendance, tardiness, and all kinds of stuff. My principal knew my family; he was from the country where my mom's oldest sister lived and where all my folks were from. So you know, privilege can work sometimes. I was a teacher's pet, sometimes too. We had an assembly that day; my elementary school went from K–6 grade. Don't you know I was called up there to show out again? I did just that, with pride. Cookie was furious with my uncle when she heard I was up on stage working out. My grandmother (Momoa) and my uncle were whooping. He remained with me until seventh grade. Another trauma.

The Veil

Do you remember the veil they say I was born with? Well, Big Mama was the first time this strange smell occurred. You know, old people can have a scent. It wasn't all the time, just a whiff every now and then. She'd (Big Mama) catch me looking at her and say, "It's going to be okay."

I would wonder, *What's going to be okay?* I told my grandmother (Momoa) about the smell, and that was where I got the idea about old people and that strange odor. After Big Momma died in '60 or '61, that strange smell came again, but this was not from an old person.

Cookie had a friend who would bring over his granddaughter every Sunday. She was one of the kindergarteners. I just loved her, and she was an only child too. She'd play with my toys and put them back in place when she finished. Now let me tell you, my favorite toy was my Thumbelina. She was the one that moved like a real baby. No one, and I do mean no one, had better touch, move, or look at her too hard because it would be hell to pay. This little girl was the exception. If my mom made the bed, she'd call me and say, "Come get your baby." No joke! As you can see, something was wrong with me too, not just Cookie. She went to church with me sometimes because we went every Sunday.

On Mondays, I would help her and the other little kindergarten class off the bus and make sure they got to their class. I was that important. I really was. You know, you love something or someone without even knowing it. It's just there. The Saturday before we went back to school, we were on the carport twirling around the poles, and I was showing her how to twirl the nation. Cookie did all that in high school, so she taught me. I mean, fire baton and all. I was showing her because I started at her age. It was so much fun, and she was smart, and as far as I was concerned, she was my little sister. On one twirl, when she went around me, that whiff came up. At first, it caught me off guard. You see, it doesn't linger; it just floats right by you, like someone with cologne who puts the wrist up just to get a whiff. I tried not to think much about it because when I hugged her as she was leaving, I didn't smell anything. Thank God, but I still told Momoa (grandmother). She just looked at me and said, "Don't worry about it." Now how can that smell be old people, and she was not even four years old?

On Monday, I was on the intercom because the kindergarten bus was late, instructing other monitors what to do. That morning, the kindergarten bus didn't come at all. I was upset because I was looking for my little sister, okay, and the other classmates too. The police came to the school, and when I saw my uncle and Momoa, I wondered, *Now what is this?* I thought Cookie was sick again, but why the police? The police were for the school, talking to the principal and other teachers, but when Momoa said she had been killed due to a car not stopping, coming around the bus, and hitting my little sister, I was devastated. I don't remember how I got home because we never really had a car we could call our own. I just know when I woke up, I was in bed with Thumbelina. I heard later that my little sister's mother was standing in the doorway, watching her cross the street, and saw the whole thing happen to my little sister. You see how trauma keeps on happening to me. No, I didn't know children died. Big Mama was the first. What kind of stuff was going on? Yes, I knew from church that Jesus died, but that was different because apparently, I didn't understand that either. Momoa told me not to worry about the whiff, but it looked like I should have.

We, Momoa, Cookie, and my uncle, moved around the corner shortly after Big Mama died. Something happened in the house; I really didn't know, but I didn't think it was because my cousin cooked my pet catfish. I caught Whiskers when I went fishing for the first time with a neighbor who lived across the street. Whiskers was still alive when we got home, so I kept him as a pet. Momoa put him in a big bread pudding pan, and I fed him a lot, but that thing grew, so they started putting him in big buckets. One of my girlfriends had an aquarium, so I felt that Whiskers needed one. Cookie wasn't having it, so the bucket was his home.

One Saturday, my cousin and I were hungry, and he could cook. He was more than ten years older than me, maybe twelve, but he was my babysitter until my uncle, who drove the milk truck, came home at noon. My cousin called me Monkey (yeah, I had a couple of those). Uncle called me Sugar Foot. By the way, he taught me to walk. Yes, sir, at nine months. You'll have to see the pictures of little Miss Brilliant. I thought I was at least two years old when I saw it. I can see I should be walking, talking, and tying my own shoes. "Are you hungry?" Of course, I was. Saturdays were grocery day, so we had to make do, and we did. My cousin asked, "Do you want some fish and fries?" Oh yeah! I came up to see where the gravy train went. Not again. I had no idea my cousin was cooking Whiskers and fries for us, but in honesty, I don't think I ever had fish and fries so good until I went to feed Whiskers the scraps of fries and pieces of bread (by the way, Whiskers was a catfish; that's how he got his name). He wasn't splashing in the bucket. He wasn't even in it. My cousin told me we ate him. I became, as they say, "sick as a dog." Whiskers and fries didn't stay down. How could someone that I loved dearly do this to me? I found out little Miss Brilliant was lacking somewhere because I didn't see that coming either.

The commotion did start that day in the house, but I don't think that was why we moved. Our house was just up the street and around the corner, so I could still see my cousin and my aunt. For the next three years, I stayed in the house.

CHAPTER 5

Momoa's Social Club

Momoa had a social club group. Those extra grandmothers were something else. They were all dolled up and went to some kind of dance too. I loved when they went to the dances because I could have the TV on. They wouldn't be at my house. I didn't care where they were. They just came around once a month, and that was plenty. Momoa would always bring back good stuff from the dances. I now think they weren't too old for all that dancing stuff. She'd say "Nothing gets old but clothes." She was happy, and so was I, for those dances.

Right before the move, the group met at our house, and two of Momoa's friends were more grandmotherly than Momoa. I'd often wonder, but now I see they doted like Cookie, just love, I guess. The whiff wanted to pay me a visit. I became standoffish toward them, and Momoa asked what was going on. Those ladies were so nice and sweet to me, and yes, I loved all those extra grandmothers. The more, the merrier. Being an only child was different. All the attention comes your way, and believe me, I loved it. I already told you, I was spoiled, rotten to the hilt. Someone always had goodies of some kind for me, but I would fetch anything they wanted and enjoy it. Sometimes Momoa would have to make me go and play because I would hang on to every word as if they were my company.

My other two favorite grandmothers were the ones I hung around the most, and I smelled the whiff again! They were at least seventy to eighty years old, I would assume. I didn't want to say anything, but I had to talk to Momoa. It didn't happen right away.

When I overheard one of them ask, "Hey, what's going on with Cookie's baby?"

Momoa said, "You know how fast these kids grow up."

Now mind you, I was not doing that much growing up from three to six months, but I didn't care what she told them. I knew a heartache for my other grandmothers was on the way. There was no point in saying something was happening to me because I couldn't explain it, or I wouldn't be able to understand. Two more funerals came and went, and again, I sure missed them.

The Move

Beginning in sixth grade, we moved to another neighborhood. Farewell to the girlfriends I'd known all my life. How was I going to survive? Don't tell me I'd make new friends because, right then, little Miss Brilliant couldn't think that far ahead. Here came the want-to-run-away-to-the-country. Remember, but you know all I know, you know that ain't happening. That lifestyle, oh no! My aunt again was in the area with my cousin. I could get to her house within a good seven to ten minutes, so it was okay.

Momoa, Cookie, and my uncle were still together. My girlfriends chatted, but I was making new friends, I'll admit. No, I wasn't over it all yet, but it was better, until one morning, my uncle hugged me. Lo and behold, I smelled the whiff. Panic got a hold of me, but I felt as if I could just close my eyes; by now, I'd joined the church and knew about the power of prayer, so God was going to hear me and fix this thing.

I was at church one Sunday in the country and had to use the restroom, which was outside. Momoa told me to come right back, but you know, I wanted water too. I knew not to try to draw water by myself from a long time ago, but…there was a man who looked just like my uncle, dressed just like him. He was a blue-jeans wearer, always had a colorful bandana, and wore a cap. My uncle was unique, and I knew it. I wouldn't trade him for anything. This man beckoned me to the well, so I thought he was going to help me get that dipper because it was really tied up. When I reached for it, the wheel that it was tied to fell down, drawing me over the edge. Just then Momoa came out and snatched me so hard (I think that was why I have neck problems now). She was going off, so the people came out of the church to see what the matter was. I tried to tell her this man, who looked like my uncle except he had red hair and beautiful blue eyes, called me over, not by name, but you know, how to use our hands to call someone over. So I went. She looked at me as if I had lost my mind. It was hot outside, but she looked at me as if to say, "This baby is having a heat stroke," and honestly, I thought I was having a stroke. No one saw him but me, but I know what I saw. By the way, when we went to the country, she fixed that; she brought water from home in those huge jars she got from working. Too bad they didn't make pampers my size because I swear I'd be in one at church. Cookie was not the queen of go-off! Momoa is!

The day we got home from church, Momoa told everybody who would listen. My other two aunts came over and our neighbors next door, down the street, and up the street, and I believe those who were in Iran, Italy, the UK, etc. I heard her say, "It's that veil." She started talking about the whiff and how everyone I told her about had died, and how I saw her dead son at the well. What? I was on the back porch. They were in the kitchen. You can't help but hear.

"What dead son?" I know all my aunts and uncles. Nobody ever mentioned anybody dead to me. So there were more secrets I didn't know. Now do you think I was going to say what happened the following Monday? That was when I prayed to God, "Let me be wrong about my uncle."

That Monday morning, I received my usual hug, remembering this as the absent daddy's replacement. The scent was faint but present. I don't think I ever hugged and held onto him so tightly in all my life. I wanted to say, "Don't leave me. Stay here. I love you so much. Please, please, please." I didn't think that would be the last time, but it was. He went to work, punched in at the time clock, suffered a stroke, and died. He was only thirty-three years old. When I came home from school, cars lined my street, and people filled our yard. I was polite and spoke, but I didn't go near where Momoa, Cookie, and the other two aunts were. I locked my door and got into bed with Thumbelina; after all, when death had visited, my uncle was always there. Now who did I have? Just alone. He had helped keep Cookie at bay. Momoa did what she could, but as I said, I was all alone. I know he didn't mean to leave.

When Cookie and my grandmother finally found out, Cookie was upset about how they had been worried since it had gotten late and I should have been home. She said I just worried her to death, and she went on and on. See, this was where my uncle would step in to stop all that, but little did I know, I wasn't alone. God was going to make everything alright. (I know he didn't mean to leave!) It just took some time.

In seventh grade, I met four other girlfriends. One had the same hole by her ear, so you know we were connected. One day, her mother asked us to go to the park to fetch her brother. Now mind you, I'd seen boys all my life, but this one, as we used to say, was "the icing on the cake," or so I once thought. If I could have had a heatstroke, that would have been the day. As school was in session, and we walked home, another ROTC cadet, whom I thought was a man—hey, I was still young and thought all people in uniform were grown men—approached us. He started running, nearly pushing me and her into the street. I almost got hit by a bus. The bus driver got out and scolded him for bothering us little girls. She said she was going to tell her brother, who would beat him up for bothering us. Well, that worked for me. The next day, her brother met us at the halfway point, and lo and behold, he was walking with the ROTC cadet. How in the world could this happen? See, if I had my uncle, he would straighten this out. The harassment didn't stop. They were laughing at us because we swore he was a man.

School was out, and wouldn't you know, this ROTC man/ boy/cadet/cousin lived on my street. After my uncle passed, Cookie decided she needed a break. She went to California to better herself and promised to send for me when school let out. She did. During that summer, the son of my aunt in the country died. I was just a few months shy of eleven, to be exact. I don't know why he never visited with his sisters. I do know he was sickly, but I heard he fell from a tree because they did all that kind of stuff, running tires on the roads that were dirt. Oh yes, I tried that; the sun tore my feet up with blisters. They could go barefoot, but not this city girl. I had to have straw hats and all. I think now they must have been laughing until the cows came home, but I was not the one and still not. You see, by now, death was no stranger to me. Honestly, I was ready to go somewhere else too, thinking death doesn't happen in California.

This soldier, cadet—boy-man, whatever—started being on my street, playing ball and carrying on. He asked my grandmother (Momoa) if he could come over as if I had invited him. If anybody was coming over, it would be the Icing on the Cake. Momoa said, "Son, she's only twelve going on thirteen. She's not taking company and is on her way to California where her mother is." Thank you, Momoa. He started cutting her yard, doing all kinds of little handy work, and she was nice. She would cook, and sometimes he would eat. Momoa made lemonade when he was doing yard work. He seemed alright. His aunt went to my church. Families knew each other. It's a small world, but the Icing on the Cake was still out there.

I hated leaving Momoa alone in the house. I just hated leaving, period. She had really been my mother ever since I can remember. Cookie was young to be my mom, by my standards then. All my other friends' moms were like my aunts in age. Cookie was eighteen when she had me, so she was young. You see, my aunt from the country was thirty-five years older than my mom. Momoa was just different; I could ask her anything, and I do mean anything. You do remember, I thought they would begin with her. She knew everything about everything. Whatever she said, that's what it was. If she said the sun was shining, and you saw rainfall, the sun was shining, and the rain would stop at some time.

"Well, Momoa, I'll see you when school's out. I'm California-bound! Here I come to California!"

California was a whole different world. I don't remember if I had heard of a taco, been to the beach, or seen a real Spanish person in my life, even though I went to school with them. I learned about ethnicity. You know, I talked a lot about the country, feeling as if I didn't live in the city back home. I had never seen a drive-in restaurant where the people are on skates, and yes ma'am, that was my first job because I can skate, believe me. I guess you could say I got cultured. I was so good in school, I skipped a grade. You know, Cookie wouldn't let me skip two grades, reasoning that she wanted me to stay with kids my own age and not be a baby graduating from high school.

When school was out, Cookie moved to Los Angeles, saying she was tired of being bossed by her brother. So I was back with Momoa for the summer, which I paid for. She said, "If you want to go back home for the summer, you'll pay your way." So you see, skating was really my ticket back to Momoa. It seemed like she would've wanted to see her mom more than me. Sure, I loved everything going on, but there's nothing like home. I got my bus ticket. My neighbors, a sweet old couple, another grandmother and grandfather watched over me like a hawk. God puts people in your life for a reason. I called them Cali Mama and Cali Papa. You know, they ate it up, and so did I. My mom's brother lived maybe a twenty-minute walk away, but they were right next door. Mom was working at night, and I still stayed by myself, but I was welcome at their house. They had grandkids my age, two of whom were great friends.

Cali Mama and Cali Papa's adult kids treated me super nicely too. They acted like I was one of their kids. We did everything: going to the beach, campfires, and you know, my namesake, the mall. I knew when they took me to the bus station, between the tears, I saw that look of worry on their face. Why? Maybe they knew what was going on with Cookie while I was at school. I do know she had an episode, and my uncle was upset. I didn't think he knew much about mental illness. He was going off worse than Momoa ever did.

Well, let me tell you, I had to show him about talking to my mom like that. They took her away for about six weeks. I could see she needed to go back home, but she couldn't. She was determined to get better; I wish I thought that way. I guess going off in this family was a hereditary trait.

While I was en route home, Cookie packed up and went to LA, where a nephew was. The country's aunt, son, and family lived there. They were nice, and we didn't live more than a ten-minute walk away.

Upon my arrival back home, there was a surprise. Momoa knew I was coming, but you know, I just wanted to see that surprise. I called her from 180 miles from home and told her when I would be there. By now, my aunt had an older man there with her, which was good, and he had a car. I'd never met or seen him and didn't really know much about him, but I knew he was older than I thought. You know, there came a time when driving was out, and if I had a license then, I'd use it. He was careful, but I was backseat driving, and I hadn't taken driver's ed yet, but God kept us all safe.

My Uncle's Last Hug

The next school term, I entered the seventh grade. One night, I stayed over at a pajama party (Cookie wouldn't let me stay anywhere. If I went across the street, down to my aunt's, one block from the house, I mean anywhere, she would be blowing the phone up every five minutes). I had a helpless baby friend who lived just across the street and one house over. Cookie would be calling and calling and calling until I would get tired and just come home. As a kid, I couldn't enjoy growing up. People would say, "She loves you, and that's why she does that."

I wanted to tell them, "Don't you love your little girls? Because when they come over, you're not blowing our phone up, and don't think she won't walk over."

It was so bad that if I went home to pee, Cookie would make me take another bath, recomb my head, and the hair I did have was not that good stuff but more down the back. But I had to pray it would stay plaited, or rubber bands wouldn't pop off, and many a day they would, so I got smart for my day not to be ruined. Whichever house I was at, I'd pee there, and their mom or big sister would get my head together. Cookie had the long wavy stuff like Big Mama. Me? Just long like Afro stuff. When Momoa would wet, oil, and brush it, you couldn't tell me anything. But if she didn't, I always heard, "Lord, have mercy." Getting back to the party, the helpless baby couldn't tie her own tennis shoes. Can you believe it? My other girlfriends and I spent half the morning teaching her, and yes, this was a part of the accelerated group. How can you be that old and can't do that? Momoa laughed herself to tears. She was happy then, and so was I.

CHAPTER 6

The Ride Home

I changed so much in a school term that Momoa didn't even recognize me at the bus station. By the way, that young man I wasn't able to take as company was there with her, dressed up in a suit, which I will never forget because I thought it was odd, being it was a Sunday, I guess. I walked right up to both of them, and they looked at me as if I was crazy or unrecognizable. When I look back, everybody was taken aback.

Now this California girl was wearing a bra, that's right, and sporting an auburn Afro so big I could hardly get on the bus, but that was the thing, hot pants and all.

I said, "Momoa, it's me."

She said, "Who you?" grabbing her purse as if I was going to rob her, and he stood up as if to protect her. I literally had to tell them who I was. She asked me, "Girl, have you had a baby?" You see, I went from a size 3 to a size 11. When I look back, I guess I would have wondered who I was too, but to me, it was a gradual change, not overnight. Mr. Suit was just shocked. He still looked the same and hadn't grown an inch, but it didn't matter because I wasn't there for him anyway. It was all about Momoa and the Icing on the Cake. I'd heard about him coming over, cutting the grass and stuff for her. I've learned to give credit where it's due.

The Icing on the Cake's sister was my best friend when I left home. Cookie would let me call twice a month, and she would call me the same way, so we kept in touch. I heard a lot about the suit wearer (nothing good), but my focal point was her older brother. His

29

sister had been saying a few things about him, but little Miss Brilliant missed a whole lifetime about him. How did that happen?

On my first day back, I had to go see her and Icing. She didn't even recognize me. No more stuffing tissue in a bra for me, and of course, I had to show her. Rocking that Afro, she was jumping up and down; after all, we're still kids, no matter that I could pass for at least fifteen, or so I thought. Her mother was, I dare say, shocked but was laughing and joking as much or maybe more than we were. Her mom was one of the nicest people I knew, even to this day. When we had school functions, her mom would give me and Cookie a ride, and since we didn't have a car, I made sure I always said thank you, so again, "Thank you" all the way to heaven.

There was a young lady and a baby on the sofa. His sister was saying who, kind of (not registering and really wasn't important at the time), even what the baby was called. I held him, jumped him some, gave him back to his mother, and continued on about Icing, and then he walked in. The earth did move, where I don't know, but it did. I was stunned in disbelief. His mom kept saying, "Guess who she is,"

Finally, he said, "I don't know who she is."

When he was told, that was the first time I got a real hug from a male who was not related to me. Yeah, yeah, yeah. I know, but this was not a lol moment. Then the bomb dropped when his mom intervened. I think now that hug was a little too long and really explained to me (at the moment, not being brilliant) who that young lady and baby were. His mom always knew I was nuts about the Icing on the Cake. I remember once he had some friends over playing basketball, and I was cheering like a professional cheerleader. I must have looked like a fool then. His sister and I talked about boys a lot, but she couldn't see my fascination with him.

I was so overwrought after she explained that I told them I had to leave, but his mom insisted he walk me home, which wasn't that far, or drive, but I chose the walk. He was going on and on, and I was much smarter back then than I seemed to be at times today. I couldn't imagine someone being so young and married with a family. You just wait. The pot can't call the kettle black. When he mentioned coming by to see me, I couldn't believe that either, but I knew enough to know better. When I went inside, what happened next was overwhelming. I must have opened up the heavens, and to this day, I really believe the angels cried with me.

The next day, you know, Momoa had me at the beauty shop to get my Afro tamed. That pressing comb had its work cut out: three hours of total misery. You know, I couldn't go to church like that. This was not California, and I don't think they were ready for that hairstyle for a woman. It had been so long since I wore a press and curl, I didn't know who I was. It was my turn to be shocked. I remember Suit came over later and told me, "Now you look like somebody I know." *Well, you're going to be saying goodbye to that girl.* Little did he or Momoa know, that I changed my ticket because I was going back in two weeks. When I went to church that Sunday and was glad to see other family and friends, I knew Icing had done me in. I was ready to leave. Momoa was so disappointed I wasn't staying all summer. I was too, but I just couldn't. All my little friends' plans were canceled. That summer was the trip I worked hard to pay for. I didn't even tell Suit goodbye. Momoa—who made me get a driver's license early—and my chauffeur went to the bus station. I boarded, cried, and kissed her goodbye, but little did I know, I'd be back soon.

CHAPTER 7

Suit Visits California (Momoa Left, She Couldn't Stay)

Suit graduated from high school and came to California. You'd think that since I didn't even say I was leaving, that would tell you something. Momoa would tell me about him from time to time; he would visit my church because his aunt went there, as did some of his neighbors and friends. Momoa once made a comment that she thought he was going to be a preacher. Well, I knew I'd never be a preacher's wife because I had too much finger-popping, doing the latest dance craze. All in all, I'm not preacher's wife material. And those types of notions were way down the road, or so I thought.

Lo and behold, he came to California, and can you believe his sister and her family lived down the street? But I didn't know then that his sister worked with Cookie. I was utterly shocked when, in the morning, I was getting in the car to drive to school—oh yes, I got a school permit (school hours only). This girl was pushing a '57 Chevy, turquoise and white. Cookie's friend, with whom we lived, was like a dad and treated me as if I were his own child. He didn't replace my uncle because no one, not even a real dad, could do that, but he was as nice as I could ask for. I know my uncle was looking down and saying, "Go ahead." When I saw him standing there (no suit), thank You, Jesus, I was floored. Momoa had said, and when he wrote, he mentioned it, but I wasn't really paying attention, I guess.

He did that old show, saying "Surprise," and boy was I surprised. I don't really like surprises. By then, I had a crush on the captain of the football team who just happened to live next door. We talked every night through the bedroom window. In the morning, we woke each other up, got dressed, and took turns driving each other to school. He had a real license, and no school hours permit. The high school wasn't that far. Sometimes we'd walk, especially when there were stores I wanted to shop at not far from home. I was learning the area. It wasn't just him; my neighbor across the street was a senior like him, and her brother was my age, just from a class behind me. If there was ever a rat pack, we were it. You mess with one, you have three more to deal with. I was having the time of my life and knew it.

Suit changed everything. Don't get me wrong. I knew from the beginning, but Cookie loved Suit. I really wasn't taking company before; the captain of the football team and other pals, male or female, were different. We hung out and spent nights together, next door I was allowed, and across the street, without her calling every minute. California might just work out, but it didn't.

Between working after school—I only went to school three hours a day. See how little Miss Brilliant was progressing? And then I worked three hours at the Burger Joint. So how much time was I having to keep company and hadn't wanted to since the Icing on the Cake?

Suit became a household fixture and really didn't seem so bad, but remember, I had heard things about him, true or untrue, but I found out the untrue was true, so there you have it. Honestly, lots of my girlfriends in California were older, and anything about anything, they knew. Cookie wasn't going to kill me, and I wasn't going to give her a reason. The thing I heard about sex was that it requires you to be in love; you have to wait for love. It was a good advice, but they missed the important part: be an adult, have a college degree, be established on your own, and make sure your partner feels like you do and has those same things and ideas as you. Now how could I do that love when Icing was taken?

Sure, I liked a lot of boys, but not like Icing. Suit was four years older than me, so he should have known something. Suit was kind of pressuring me, but deep down, I knew. I wanted to blame everybody because nothing went like the movies. I'd seen enough of them to get the general idea, but this wasn't it. Icing.

One day after school, Cookie was having a rage thing with the man who was as close to a father as I've ever had, besides my uncle. He was a jealous man, but in a nutshell, he really was too old for Cookie, by at least thirty years. He didn't want anyone to look at her twice, but she was gorgeous, a perfect little soda bottle. Everybody would look at her more than twice. I used to have to tell my male friends, "That's my mama," and they couldn't believe it. I was so proud to tell the world that.

They always asked, "Is she Black?" I guess with the hair and all that, the coloring of a Jamaican, so I guess I see why. Suit was even shocked when he met Cookie.

I know when I was in the sixth grade, I was taller than she was. She was packing our bags and said we were leaving because she was tired of this. I begged her, "Let's not leave." It was two months until school was out, and I didn't want to leave my new world again.

I knew Cookie was on the edge, so I called Momoa, and she said, "I'm on the way." My cousin and uncle in California stayed in the house with me until Momoa got there. The man who treated me like his own moved out until we left. Another thank you to the heavens.

Getting Cookie back home was a difficult trip on the bus. I wish Momoa had let her son drive us back because when we got 180 miles from home, the bus driver had to call for help and an ambulance, which took Mama and Momoa the rest of the way home. There I was again, on my own. Our main belongings had been boxed up and sent home, but we still had luggage, so I handled that. Suit was still in California, where I wish he had stayed. I called a cab from the bus depot and got to Momoa's house because I won't ride with the chauffeur again.

Cookie was on the tenth floor. That's what they called it before they sent you to the asylum if that didn't work. She (Cookie) was there for about two to three weeks. I had to start school at the end of the year, but I still only took three classes. I came home with plenty of credits, but these I needed in this state to graduate. My family knew the principal, so I'd take these three, and when school started, I would be a senior, take the rest of the three to finish up, and be completed before January, and wouldn't come back except to graduate with the class in May. Tell me God ain't good!

Well, shortly after returning home, I began to feel sick every day, all day, and was glad I only had a few hours of class a day. You know, Momoa said she thought I was pregnant, and I and Cookie said no because I didn't miss the cycle. Momoa said, "Something is wrong with this child," so we went to the doctor, and he said I was exactly what she thought. The dilemma was no cycle was missed, so there we were. He thought maybe this baby could be born in November, but they'd have to be careful because they're not sure. So every three weeks, I was at the ob-gyn. Suit claimed he wanted to marry me, but I still didn't want to marry him. I told Momoa why not, and she understood. It was not about Icing. He was cheating with the girl he left behind because I saw them when he thought I was in class, but I was out earlier than he knew. It looked like the minute we got back, he was not that preacher after all. Cookie and I couldn't tell her because, at that point, he could have owned six churches, seven hospitals, and ninety laundromats. I wasn't going to marry this man. Like she said, "So help me, God."

In May, I noticed Momoa had the whiff, but everything, including the water, smelled odd. The whiff was so unpleasant that I moved back to my own bedroom. Yes, I wanted to sleep with Momoa, especially since Cookie was in the hospital, and I deeply loved her and missed her. She told me, "I'm not going to let you marry that boy. He had me fooled too."

On the final Sunday, the last time she attended church because the following Sunday would be her funeral, we walked home in the July heat. Well past her eighties, she asked an aunt for a ride home because the chauffeur had died a few weeks after we returned. However, the aunt said her car was full, so Momoa and I set out on foot. Only God knows how we didn't succumb to that heat, but we made it to a little corner store. She got her favorite drink, and I got mine. The store owner, familiar with our family, asked why we were walking in the heat. She advised us to wait for her delivery truck to return, but Momoa said we were almost home. The store owner seemed slightly upset about our situation. Momoa asked her to wet her handkerchief, which she always carried, and the storekeeper gave me a wide-brimmed straw hat, which I promised to return, and I did. Momoa was physically fit, no doubt. She could outwalk me any day, but not this time.

The Saturday before she passed, we had a talk; she sensed the whiff was on me. Maybe that's why she inquired about my return to my own bedroom, but I didn't admit that. I mentioned being sick a lot and waking up throughout the night as the reason, which was partly true. Momoa knew I was really afraid of dead people. She used to say, "They can't hurt you."

I would respond, "But they can make you kill yourself."

She would laugh heartily at that, making me laugh too. This woman was my world. At fifteen years old, I knew that if I could sacrifice my life for hers, I would do so in a heartbeat, without hesitation. She was my everything. She used to call me "Monkey" or "little Miss Brilliant" and told me she wouldn't come back to this world for anything. "I'm going to see Jesus, so don't be scared," she said. I didn't believe in ghosts, but I always had strange dreams and could talk about things I should know nothing about. She would tell me to wait until sunrise so they wouldn't come true. I don't know if that was to calm me down, but those dreams eventually became reality.

The Sunday after our walk home from church, Momoa suffered a stroke. Thankfully, no lawsuit. The next-door neighbor, having just seen Cookie leave to buy cigarettes, helped transport her to the hospital. I'm grateful to those neighbors.

After phone calls were made, people from California, Texas, and other places came home, taking turns visiting the hospital. Cookie was distraught, so much so that they readmitted her to the psychiatric ward on the tenth floor. When I asked to go, all I heard was, "You don't need to stay here." So around 2:00 a.m., while the house was asleep, I put on Momoa's big sombrero and walked to the hospital alone. I wasn't always wise, but this was about Momoa. Rain, shine, sleet, or snow, nothing was going to stop me.

I was underage to visit that ward alone, but I claimed I had an ob-gyn appointment, and it worked. That was a horrendous walk. If I had been further along, I might have gone into labor. I definitely wasn't walking back. Upon my arrival, I encountered two aunts who were upset with me, which I understand now, but at that moment, it didn't matter. My mother, Cookie, was in the hospital, and Momoa, the other part of my world, was gone.

When God puts you on a mission, there's a reason. That day, July 15, was my mom's birthday, and coincidentally, my uncles, born two years apart, shared the same birthday. It's ironic.

When I saw Momoa, I was shocked. They kept saying she was doing fine and getting better, but what I saw was worse than a hospital scene in a TV show. A nurse came in, and I asked her if she could unhook some tubes because I needed to talk to Momoa, and I needed her to talk to me, just for a minute. She said it was time to change a tube, but Momoa couldn't hear me anyway. I understood what a coma meant, but in my mind, they didn't know Momoa and me; they didn't have a clue.

As God is my witness, I got to the foot of her bed and pulled back the sheets just to rub her feet, the same feet I rubbed when she took me to a huge amusement park in Texas with a broken foot. While packing our lunch, and most of the church's too, she dropped a plate on her foot. It swelled, and she iced it, thinking she would be okay. Well, she wasn't. Her foot and leg became so swollen. I remember, at the age of six or seven, in the seventh grade, finding the emergency center. They rushed out, and Momoa was almost unconscious. Panic set in, and I knew we were in trouble. The church was on this trip, but she made me stay close to her. Oh yeah, I still had fun because I only wanted to ride two rides and eat all day. I remember them getting a wheelchair for her and gathering information from me about the bus number, church, names of my aunt, and other adult church members. Trust me, the whole four busloads showed up. Momoa was sick; she tried to pretend, but I had never seen her like that. They had her foot all wrapped up. They put all of us little kids on a Greyhound so the bigger kids could stay, but that was alright with me. I was ready to go and had to take care of Momoa.

I noticed her feet were cold to the touch, so I figured my hands would warm them up. So I rubbed them in an upward motion like I used to do when she got off from work to soak her feet. I remember saying, "Momoa, it's me. I had to come see you and tell you I love you."

Momoa sat up in bed, opened her eyes, and said, "There my baby is," then laid down and left this world.

At that moment, I knew I needed God to come down from heaven and help me. When I came to, I was in a hospital bed myself. Momoa was lying an arm's distance away, looking more beautiful than ever. What in the world was going on here? Somebody, anybody, please help me.

My uncle, cousins, and crew arrived shortly in mass hysteria, and yes, I was at the top of the list. The nurse kept asking who I was, and finally, she recognized me as being Cookie's baby. Everyone seemed to have forgotten about Cookie until that moment. The question arose: "Who's going to tell her?" Since my uncle was there, Cookie's oldest brother went to the psychiatric ward and spoke to her doctor; he thought maybe. My uncle and I tried to tell Cookie, and I have seen her at her lowest, but that day, the sound that escaped her was something that had been cooped up in her whole life. I saw right then how my mom's life had been. She was a fragile woman, she felt alone, and the world she knew was alien to her. She kept repeating, "My mama is not dead," over and over until they came to sedate her. It made me snap out of it. What in the world? During the week of the funeral, Cookie was still in psychiatric care. They let her out with two nurses. I'm sure she didn't even know who she was, where she was, or who I was. She just kept saying "Mama" until I had to get up and hold her like she was my baby, and from that day on, Cookie became my baby. Bye, Momoa. I love you always!

CHAPTER 8

Growing Up Little Miss Brilliant

While Cookie was still in the psychiatric ward and everyone had returned to their normal life, I had a new norm. I was left in the house alone, fending for myself. I didn't realize how many things I knew how to handle. Momoa had left me a stash hidden in the house for emergencies, and if this wasn't the time, I didn't know what would be.

Cookie finally came home but wasn't really there. It was hard to see someone like that. Growing up was going to be swift for me. God instilled in me the strength to not break, to stay strong, and to cry if I must, but to understand that all was not lost.

School started in September. I had my firstborn son in October and went back to school after Thanksgiving break, staying until Christmas break. I had enough credits. That summer, I had to marry Suit. By then Cookie was better but not about that. Poncho, as he was called, was nine months old by now. By the summer of '71, Suit was going into the military. Cookie insisted that the baby needed a name, that father thing. Well, I returned to school for the months of September to November, taking required classes for the state I now lived in. By the way, I was driving my very own little blue bug (Volkswagen) that my grandfather needed to sell. I couldn't drive it at first because it was a stick shift. Suit didn't want me to learn how, but with all the yelling and name-calling, who could learn? But you know, where there's a will, there's a way. Before he left, he and Icing gave me driving lessons, believe it or not. As I said, he was really married, to a total of three kids, and all was well. I was no longer some dazed cheerleader on the verge anymore.

While Suit was at basic training, I went and got my driver's license. With my baby in the back seat, I went to get the license and took the test, and the tester asked me who was with me. Shocked, I said, "No one, just me and the baby."

Next, he asked, "Whose baby?"

"Mine, you know." He looked at me as if I were kin to Cookie.

I was already breaking the law with no license, permit, or anything, and owning a vehicle. So you see, God was with me right then. He asked me to leave the baby with a tester and said, "Show me what you can do." We got in that little blue VW, hit the road, and parked at the fairgrounds, where the driving test was. My biggest problem was doing hills, but trust me, I was ready to roll with that clutch to keep the car from stalling and rolling back into someone else's car. I wasn't expecting to get into real traffic, but that's what we did.

We went and got burgers and even went to his house, met his wife and kids, took him back to work, and got that real license. No permit, because, as I explained, I had a job after school and needed my car since Suit was at basic training. The bus took too long; I and the baby needed to get around, and I couldn't keep waiting for six weeks in case of an emergency.

My new best friend gave me that real license, buckled the baby in the car, and off I drove. He was shaking his head as I pulled off, waving.

When Suit came back, saying he was at the bus station and was going to call a cab, I told him his ride was on the way. When I drove up, taking every hill on the road and going out of my way to get home, instead of being proud, the ranting and raving started. I no longer needed him to take me everywhere. I opted for this; my grandfather took me to the finance company and put just my name on it. Alone, my name. My grandfather had always been the cosigner. This car belonged to my sister, my twin, but she got married, moved away, and couldn't afford it. The job she had was supposed to have been a transfer; she was a plant manager, but once she got there, they claimed she couldn't pass the physical test. So he was stuck with her car. So you see, God was there again.

Suit went on to the place they drafted him to. I went on and marched with my class. On graduation night, I turned sixteen. My baby boy and I strode proudly across that stage, and I did have a cheering section of family. Many of my classmates didn't even know who I was because I wasn't there with them. Remember, I got skipped a grade in California, so my classmates were a year behind me. I attended school from September until November, taking gym, English IV, political science, and other mandatory classes. Can you believe my gym teacher taught my mother, who was a cheerleader, then a majorette, at the school I graduated from? When she showed me her pictures in the trophy cases, I cried. I hadn't even noticed them at all. I said, "Go ahead, Cookie." The woman was a knockout. As my baby boy grew up, and I showed him his grandmother in the trophy case, we were floored. I guess that was her happy time before I came along, but when you really look at the photos, there's still a haunting, lonely look.

I remained married to Suit for fifteen years. He came back home from overseas duty with all his international conquests to show the world, including me. Why people like to flaunt that kind of stuff, I've never figured out. It's hard enough trying to continue with a marriage, but at sixteen years old, I knew this wasn't how it was supposed to go. Momoa's idea of him being a preacher went right out the window.

Stormy weather was just the beginning. Suit had shown me his true colors earlier, and I thought I was going to be stuck like this for the rest of my life. I pleaded, "Say it ain't so. Please, Momoa, help me." I had a praying grandmother (Momoa), and I was asking her to please ask God to help me. Oh, I was asking Him myself, but I just figured she had more powerful prayers since she was up there with Him. Prayers availeth much, I do know that.

You'd think once you get grown and try to move on your own, that's when the real troubles start. Two other children were born; I got myself a good job, and Suit landed a couple of really good jobs but wouldn't stay on them. Mistreating the kids was something I couldn't tolerate. My mother, Cookie, wasn't a constant beater of me, so I wasn't going to take that from Suit. He totaled out cars I kept buying through my credit union and drew unemployment that I didn't even know about, and that's when the biggest actual fight started. Blowing rent money with his friends, after the last physical fight, little Miss Brilliant decided, "I'm an adult now (avenging angel), and I don't care what Mama Cookie says. It's time." She didn't really know how bad it was because I needed someone I could talk to, and she wasn't it. I didn't want to worry her anyway. That last fight put me in the hospital, so there was no way I could fake and shake this off. Mouth wired up, crutches the whole nine yards. Luckily, I had a hell of a supervising chief who got me to a department where I didn't have to chatter a lot.

You know when a six-year-old starts pulling out a butter knife and tells you not to hit his mama anymore, you've crossed the line. This same six-year-old came home, and his eye was nearly out of its socket. He said Suit elbowed him because he was trying to cut his hair (sideline barber), and he wouldn't sit still. He almost lost his eye, so after that eye surgery, the avenging angel was out to kill. You know, I'm going to have to tell you about this real situation sooner than later.

Divorce was on the horizon, then I found out about Suit cosigning with some woman. He had no job, so community property. The state told me I would have to pay. What! So now, I lost my apartment and, by the way, I moved in with Cookie. Can you believe that? She was talking about his childhood and feeling sorry for him when he almost killed me! After my grandmother died, my mother (Cookie)'s siblings didn't want to let her have the house. Each one of them had their own home, but the only one that wanted her to have it was the aunt in the country. You know how family can be, so that's how she ended up in the projects. Lord. have mercy. My cousin and I had to kick Suit out, and God knows I had to move into a one-bedroom.

Project Havoc

I acquired another full-time job. Thank You, Jesus! It helped me survive and tackle a $30,000 debt owed to Suit's friend. My schedule was eight to five at one job, and six thirty to twelve thirty at the other. Eventually, it improved to eight thirty to twelve thirty at one job, and 2:00 p.m. to 10:00 p.m. at the next, while trying to pick up my kids from school, help with homework, and attend night classes. On Mondays, I had a course at a campus. One night, after parking my new car, someone vandalized it the next morning. They stripped the antenna, threw paint on it, and knifed my bucket seats. The insurance company was not pleased. Since I hadn't had the car for three days, when I got it back, I would stay a few hours with an aunt who lived nearby, then wake up at 5:00 a.m. to return to Cookie and my children. You do what you must, and with God's help, I managed.

My career job went on strike, but not me. I was labeled a scab and many other things, but I didn't care what they called me; I was determined to make enough money to leave the projects. I explained the situation to my other job's boss, who assured me that my job would await my return. Thirty days of working during the strike enabled me to move out with my three musketeers, forever changing their lives, especially my baby girls. Born with sickle cell anemia, she and her siblings never really had a father, even forty years later. They recount horrific stories of their father's abuse: locking them outside all day, forcing them to eat from dumpsters, and enduring beatings. It's unbelievable they never told me; they were too scared.

Each one was relieved when he left. My son, now forty-seven, once told me about a time when his father, whom he calls by his first name, brutally beat his brother over a toy, despite a six-year age difference. He recalled his dad jumped on his brother with his knees in his back, stripping him naked, and nearly beating him to death. He could hear all that was going on and punching him all on his head and everything. He said he knew when he got older, his dad was going to do to him the same thing. After he had beaten him an inch from his life, he went to the sofa and smoked, and as he laid his head back, he thought about getting a kitchen knife and slit Suit's throat.

This child was no more than seven years old and thought like that. I was afraid cause its coming for him. He told me he prayed for our marriage to end, fearing he would end up in jail for the beatings. To this day, he shares these horror stories. When I ask his siblings, they confirm, revealing more stories I never knew. I questioned my parenting, wondering how my children were too frightened to confide in me. Maybe this story would be different if told from a prison cell. He felt treated like garbage. To this day, I wonder how things are, but I've moved past these issues only through prayer and mercy. I pray he can too.

We eventually moved to our own apartment. I resumed my previous routine, which was challenging but an improvement. I kept the musketeers in their original schools that had me and them really running but after school was out, for a while, then transferred them to schools near our new home. This change was a blessing.

No child support came; I stopped taking time off from my job for court. Why miss money when they already know he was in arrears? Can you believe one day the company took us to lunch and, lo and behold, there he was, working as a waiter? But let him tell it, he's broke. I decided he wasn't going to get away with this. Well, the court date came; he did appear and told the judge he wanted the car, which I paid for. Yes, I took the furniture; it was mine too. He told the judge he had no job, and I had specifically told them where he worked. Oh, by the way, he was out the next day.

The courtroom thought this was a joke. He asked how he was going to pay the car note from her credit union, which would come directly out of her check, and leave her stranded with two jobs and three children. "Tell me, sir, how does that work?" The pitchfork was on standby (lol); by the way, my choice of weapon is the flamethrower. If I'd had access to either one, I would be in prison today for annihilating a parish courthouse. You see, I'm proving to you that God lives.

It really was a waste of time and did no good, but I and the musketeers survived. You do know the best way to get revenge is to *survive*! While he was standing there looking idiotic, I knew trouble doesn't last always.

Years passed. He would call the kids, saying he was going to take them here and there. I'd call home, and they'd still be waiting. He did show up once to take them to a festival. Give credit where credit is due. I noticed whenever he tried to make a date, if I didn't want to be around, he'd no-show. So I guess I was to blame, but he was not a family man trying to rekindle things.

Cookie was still having issues. When she wasn't in the hospital, my little baby genius was. I remember just once, I asked him to stay so I could go home, shower, and check on the boys. He came to the hospital and called me, saying he "couldn't stand to see her like that again." He never helped out, however; I got through it anyway. I would take vacation time between her and Cookie, so I'd still get paid.

God is an awesome wonder. I look back and see the goodness of it all. Sometimes I would vacay on one job, and then I'd just have one job to work. People used to say, "I don't know how you do it." Answer: "May's Baby." Be blessed, Suit.

CHAPTER 9

Love for Cookie

Since Momoa passed, my mama never really recovered. As I tried to raise myself and her, you know, God stepped in. Fifteen was horrendous. Momoa kept me from being really alone, and to this day, fifty-two years later, she's still there when I get to the loneliest times of my life.

Cookie (Mama) was a generous woman. Maybe five feet two inches on a good day, her skin was the beautiful color of deep chocolate, and she had the figure of a perfect little soda. Without permission, I don't think I can name it, but it's my favorite today and really popular. God's creation. Beautiful hair. When she wanted it straight, she would go to the hair salon to get it blown out or take it to the ironing board herself. There's a first time for everything. When I saw her do that, you know, I thought she was really sick, but she was rocking long straight hair like Big Mama. You know, I noticed she looked like a replica of Big Mama; she didn't look anything like her mother, but neither did I.

Cookie was the baby of her siblings. Her older sister was thirty-five years older than she was. Yep, can you imagine? Cookie would tell me stories about her growing up with her nieces and nephews, but they never obeyed her. How could they? She was four, so she couldn't boss anybody. We would laugh at all the things they did growing up in that time and space. She was so happy. I really believe that she was truly happy back in the day. She was full of glee, and I too seeing her like that, but it only lasted until the stories were over. Oh, I wish we could stay in the room of glee. She loved it there. If I could, I would abracadabra and keep her there, except make her an adult. Or just so, if remaining a child would keep her happy, I would be willing to forgo being born to see my mama like that. There was joy in just knowing she could get to that point because to see her that way was amazing. I could only imagine what life with this Cookie would be like.

Mental illness is not something I would wish on anyone, and trust me, the flamethrower had plenty of enemies, but even I would have to tell them to drop and roll to put the flames out. See, I didn't turn out too bad. Cookie would say, "Monkey, you should be ashamed of yourself," when I was bad, but I wasn't, only if it caused her sadness, so I would try to be good.

I miss this mama of mine. I missed her even when she was here on this side. Being told when I hear people say being absent in the body and present with the Lord, in all honesty, hadn't really worked for me. I do try consoling myself, but after thirty-five years, I'm still calling on the Lord to help see me through, and He's made it better, so I'm really trying to do my part. You know, God is a busy man, but for sure, He always takes the time for me whenever I call, and trust me, that's a lot.

This book could have been all about Cookie, but it would be a tearjerker, and I'm not having that. I guess you wonder why I do a lot of referring to her as Cookie, and now it's time for my secret to tell you. When I say Cookie, I could smile about her, but when I go to Mama, I couldn't muster my tears.

CHAPTER 10

A Little Love Lesson—
She Got Her Wings

Delory Dell Jackson is who Cookie is—my mother, in real life, whom I would not trade for anything, even if I had to repeat what we went through. She was the baby of her family, born thirty-five years after her oldest sister. She had nieces and nephews born a few months after she was. I always asked her, "Why don't they do what you say?"

She told me, "I'm the same age as them, so you can't make them mind you."

True. I thought that was the funniest thing because once she told me how my uncle in the country spanked her and his son for throwing dirt on each other, and I said, "How could he whip his sister-in-law?"

The reply was, "I was three years old, and his son was two years old. We were just babies, but I can remember that spanking." He's the uncle who shot the (baby) mule in the head, so I know for sure that whipping your little sister-in-law, you're deranged for sure, way before the mule incident. How we laughed.

Mama had very, very few laughing moments, but she had the prettiest smile and dimples. This mama of mine could turn heads wherever she went. I picked up on that early in life. I was proud to call her my mama, even when she was at the mental asylum on the tenth floor. No matter what, Cookie was the best she could be.

Sorrow took hold of me for her because it knew her soul was unhappy. I myself have to fight a lot of times from going into despair, but who doesn't from time to time? She just couldn't stay. I wished so much happiness for her, but it didn't come until she told my daughter, who was around eleven years old whom we'll call Baby Genius, that her mother was coming with her baby brother to take her home on the chariot. Baby Genius had never heard of Cookie's name or Cookie's brother, so when she asked me about them, I told her about the pictures I had, and another aunt had of Cookie's (Momoa) mom. She said that grandma was crying, and Baby Genius was upset too, and to be honest, I was torn up from the floor myself. Little did I know that in less than a week, Cookie would be leaving me.

You always think when people are sick, death is lurking. I'd taken off from one of my two jobs for a doctor's appointment myself. Oh well, I couldn't tell Mama I wasn't at my best to worry her, but when I went to get my paycheck, my supervisor told me that an aunt of mine had called and said my mom was sick, and I needed to come and take her to the doctor. When I arrived at her apartment, one sister was there, and she left her, I just remember her saying how "sick and tired" she was of Cookie. Well, she didn't have to be sick and tired much longer; she left me to get her to the hospital, and that was that.

Of all days, I was having car trouble, to be fixed the next day, but I had someone with me who helped me get her to the hospital. I asked her if she got the whiff of my mama. She said no, but I did, and it was strong. She drove me to the hospital, and I told her I would call her. Mama looked odd to me, and now I know what was happening. They had her in a wheelchair. One cousin who worked there came by to check on us to see what was happening. We were still waiting three hours later. The cousin's daughter came by, and I asked her where her grandmother was, which was my mom's other sister, and she said she was going to get her hair done. She had just dropped her off because she worked there too. It was just me and Cookie alone, as usual. It was funny how the worst day of your life can replay in your mind as if it's taking place right now.

Finally, we were called to a room in the back. I sat on the examining table and turned Mama (Cookie) to face me, and her eyes seemed strange in color. Before we went to the exam room, I left Cookie for just a moment to go to the restroom myself because I wasn't at my best. No longer than a minute later, when I got back, I asked her if they had called her name. She said no.

You know older people, not that Cookie was old exactly at fifty-two years old, but she didn't always correct people. She would answer to the name Delray, and I would always say, "Mama, tell them the correct pronunciation of your name and the spelling too." To this day, I want to blame this mistake for her death, but I know God doesn't make mistakes by a name slipup.

There was another girl sitting next to me and Cookie with her mom; they were there because her mom had a splinter in her finger. When I saw her hand, it was really infected. So I was thinking they were just going to treat it. You know, of all days, her mom's name was Delray, and her mom was born in the same area as my mother. They were seven miles from each other. I don't know how old her mom was, but she seemed much older than Cookie. We started talking about our moms; they have the same last names. We knew some of the same people from down in the country, so we just knew we were related.

While on my bathroom trip, when I came back, I asked Cookie if they had called her name, and I noticed the new cousin was gone with her mom. When I asked Cookie about them, she said they were going to admit her mom. The finger did look bad, so I thought nothing of it but hoped I'd see her again (be careful what you wish for).

While in the examining room, I really noticed Cookie's eyes. I took off her glasses and wiped them so I could look at them up close. She'd never had light brown eyes before. I was sitting there, wondering what in the world was going on, when she suddenly started wetting herself. Thankfully, I always pack a change of clothes for her. I called for a nurse to help me, and lo and behold, the nurse who came in was a classmate of mine.

When she entered, she said, "I didn't know this lady was your mom. She's here all the time." I wasn't surprised. Cookie was always going to the hospital for one thing or another, whether it was a real symptom or not. The nurse mentioned that Cookie was just here two days ago, complaining of chest pains, but I don't know what happened after that. "If I had known she was your mom, I would have looked after her myself," she said. We exchanged numbers so that next time something would go wrong or when she would come here, I would be on it. By the way, this was a charity hospital, but no excuses should be made.

We showered Mom up, and the doctor talked to her and took her blood for bloodwork, the whole nine yards. She complained of indigestion and lots of other ailments. He said he only saw a little infection, gave her a prescription, and told us if she wasn't feeling better by Monday to come back. This was on Friday. While I was looking at her, I constantly reminded myself to say, "I love you." I know she knew I did, but I don't remember when I last told her verbally.

I called my ride, and we took Cookie home. I drove my vehicle to my house, scared every minute it would cut off and not start. I couldn't wait until the next day to get it fixed. I made it home in one piece (thank You, Jesus). My oldest child said that my aunt had called and asked me to call her. I hesitated to call because she couldn't wait to get away from me and Cookie. I thought and told my son she just wanted to know what the doctor said, but she could have gone with me and known for herself. When I did call, a friend of hers answered the phone. I told him who I was, and he said they had to take my mom back to the hospital, repeating it over and over. I said, "I just left the hospital. You're mistaken."

He insisted, "No, they got something mixed up and called her to come back." What?

I remember lying across the bed and must have fallen asleep, but I woke up to Cookie calling my name. She said, "Monkey."

I sat straight up in bed and replied, "What, Ma dear?" I looked at the clock; it was midnight, and the room was pitch-black. The phone hadn't rung because I put it in bed with me to be sure to hear it. If the kids were up, they always answered the kitchen phone. I asked them if the phone had rung; they said no. They were having a sleepover, and I know they were up all night and wouldn't miss a phone call.

I got up and dressed, called my friend, and told her what had happened. We agreed she'd get her brother, and they would drive in case my car stopped. He'd then take my car to fix the alternator. Sure enough, my car stopped a short distance from my apartment, but they were coming, so I wasn't worried. I got into her car, and he took mine. Off to the hospital we went. She dropped me at the emergency room, but the doors wouldn't open, so I told her I'd just walk around to the front of the hospital's main entrance. The ER was on the far side, and I thought that's where they were. Still, no phone call had come.

As I rounded the corner across the street, I walked directly into the path of an eighteen-wheeler. I knew something bad had happened when I came around the corner. The driver got out of his truck, screaming and yelling, and so was I. Two figures were sitting out front on a kind of flower bed in front of the building, and I screamed and hollered even more. The driver was holding me upright as the figures approached us, and then I recognized who they were. One was my aunt, and the other was her daughter, who had checked on us earlier while we were waiting to see the doctor.

My aunt and cousin asked who had called me, and I said no one. I didn't know why I was screaming and hollering, but I knew. The driver came into the hospital with us. I had another classmate who worked there in the psych ward, which I didn't know. We were best friends in the seventh grade (the one who told me there was no Santa). There was an attendant with her, another classmate, but I had graduated high school with him. It had been so long since we'd seen each other. They said they'd heard me screaming and hollering from the tenth floor of the building. Seeing me really struggling with the man trying to get me across the street, they thought I must be a patient needing to be admitted. they got downstairs and realized it was me, and I was still screaming and hollering, unable to stop myself. When my classmates saw my family, especially my seventh-grade pal, she found out what had happened by my aunt, who used to live around the corner from her, who happens to be Icing's sister.

I thought I was screaming and hollering, but another girl was going off, which made me shut up. We were all looking at each other, and then I recognized her—the new cousin. They had admitted her mom under my mom's real name by default of paperwork. When they admitted her to the ICU and gave her mom my mom's heart medicine, it killed her mom.

One of the nurses, who used to live right next door to us, saw the error; that's why they called to bring my mom back. The lady who had died was supposed to get the infection prescription and go home, but instead, you see what happened.

When they called my mom to come back, she called my aunt. They rushed her back and said they would admit her immediately, but they did while they were trying to get the paperwork right, figuring out who was who.

My mom died in the admitting room with all those people looking at the chaos. My mom kept saying she was having indigestion, so she asked my aunt to get her a Coke, and she did. She said Mama (Cookie) took a swallow, burped, and said, "Don't call Monkey," and those were the last words she spoke. So you see, when I told them she called out my name at twelve o'clock, that's exactly when she left me. To this day, I tell anyone that Cookie, Mama, the truly deep love of my life, called my name ever so gently before she left for me to hear her. At that precise time, I was the last thing on her mind. Say what you will, I've got to get into heaven because a true love of mine is waiting for me, and I know she is.

My aunts fought over who told me, and I told them no one did. The hospital had security in the room where she was and where they took her, and they wouldn't let me see her for myself to believe she was gone, but maybe it was for the best. The week of her passing, I called everyone, and I went by her house like I did every day when I was working, and she'd be sitting on her little porch, so I could wave on the way to the first job so I could see her. No, I was off from work for two weeks, but I just knew they'd made a mistake until the funeral was really over.

I regretted not saying to her how much I loved her so she could hear those words, not what was in my mind for her. So on the day of the wake—Lord have mercy—after we got through that, I was asleep, and I dreamed that we were back in that examining room. But this time, we were both sitting on that table, swinging our feet like fishing from a pier. That room was lit up as bright as the OR at the hospital, and I said, "Mama, you know I love you."

She said, "I love you too," and kissed me full on the lips.

Never ever let a day go by without telling your loved ones that you love them. That taught me a lesson I'll never forget.

I always called Cookie "Mam" or "Ma dear," so I'm saying to the extreme love of my life, "I love you, and ta-ta for now."

CHAPTER 11

Until

On Mother's Day 2023, I let Cookie fly. It took thirty-five years for me to let her go with love. You know me by now, but the crazies just kept me from really letting go. Yes, I had accepted it, but I was still holding on, yearning so deep inside that Mother's Day was a chore for me. And yes, I do have three children of my own, but that couldn't fix this, no matter how I tried to spin the tale.

"Monkey," I know that's what she'd say. "What's wrong with you? I'm free from this world." But I wanted her here with me, no matter what. This kind of grief haunted me until I glammed up for the first time since 2019. I had been makeup-free since COVID; no one really sees you all masked up anyway, so why bother? But getting ready for church that particular day, it was like (excuse me), I said, "Put on those big girl panties, and show me what you're working with"—no more pampers.

When I got myself together, I almost forgot how. What stared back at me was Cookie herself. I had never ever thought there was any resemblance of her wasted on me, but lo and behold, ta-da.

I walked into the church, and there was no dragging and no hating this day of all days. After church, I'd never felt a Mother's Day like this one. Don't think I didn't ask God for any help. Leaving the house, driving to church, getting inside, you'd have thought I was going to get executed, but well, well, well.

Cookie's favorite entertainer just recently died, and I said, "Tell Cookie I said hello," because I know she's up there singing with you. You two girls rock.

So, Mama, I'll untie those wings so you can finally fly. My heart feels better than it ever has about your absence, but they say love never dies, and I see why. I'm not going to chain you here anymore with me.

So go ahead, Cookie, fly away and be happy. Monkey is okay!

CHAPTER 12

People You Thought You Knew

Talking about the wolf in sheep's clothing, don't be fooled. If you stay on the path of the shepherd, you won't get devoured. Don't stray; stay on the course.

Be not dismayed when betrayal comes—and it will. Just *keep on living*. That's Momoa talking. She used to say I didn't have any friends (and I'd be saying to myself, "I have a world full of them. She doesn't know what she's talking about")—just lots of acquaintances, which was so true.

My list could be endless, but the most important one on this list was myself. What I called betrayers were the ones little Miss Brilliant allowed to tell her stories (liars, promise breakers, just perfect deceivers) for no earthly reason, those who stole my heart away, but now I know, "He will heal the brokenhearted and bind up their wounds."

You know that whiff thing going on? I wish it worked about giving a heads-up to the living experience that brings down doom and despair, but I realize the whiff couldn't be fixed or altered. But this living thing, you can change. The battered can and will heal. In the end, you'll get to the path that leads to being content in whatever state you find yourself. Live your best life! Life just watches out for a few, I tell you.

CHAPTER 13

The Flamethrower— Millionaire Friend

I've mentioned my choice of weapon being the flamethrower, but only on special occasions when needed.

A girlfriend from high school became the sister I never had. All my girlfriends have been like that to me. I guess being an only child left me with that flaw. I've loved them all dearly and still do. Throughout my first marriage, I had struggles, and one friend, before she went to the military, was always there. In high school, she stayed with me a lot and wore my clothes—oh yes, the girl was a fashion plate. She comes from a rather large family, but they are the best people in the world. Her mother worked hard to provide for them.

Once, when I was leaving school to go to work, I saw her at the bus stop. We had gym together, and I asked her where she was going. Her sweater was wrapped around her; she had had an accident and needed to go home. She lived not far from where I worked part-time as a salesgirl and modeled on the side. I said, "Hop in." She showed me where she lived, introduced me to her family, and I asked her how she got to school. She had to catch two city buses and told me how early she had to get up. I was shocked because I could walk to school in a good twenty-five minutes. I used to do that, but since I had the VW and a job, I drove.

I asked Cookie if she could stay the week at the house with us, and she said it was okay. Cookie met her mom; like I said, she was like a big sister to me. She helped out with my first musketeer, and he was crazy about her. I didn't have to worry so much with her at home with him. We rocked that hall at school. We wore the same size clothing, and she was tall like me. We used to go to her church in the country. She had no car either. Cookie, the first musketeer, her mom, and me. Like I said, this is what family does.

After graduation, she enlisted in the military, went overseas, came back, got a good job, and worked part-time. Yes, she came back with a plan. We didn't see much of each other, but I always knew the times she'd help me out financially. I have to give credit where it's due. Thank You, Jesus.

One day out of the blue, she asked me about Icing, yes, the Icing I mentioned earlier. She saw him at least three days a week. She said he was always coming from the gym. That's more than I knew about him, and he was my neighbor. By now in life, he had children, and so do I. He and Suit were friends. I never really saw him much. I worked evening hours, and he and Suit had day hours when Suit was working. I told her I couldn't and wouldn't set that up, but if she happened to come over one day, and he was there, I would introduce him. If you don't introduce people, that's rude, but I won't partake in anything else. She did occasionally drop by, but she wasn't a fan of Suit, nor was he of her. The meeting never took place, as far as I know. Whenever I visited home, I never failed to see her and her mother. I moved away more than twenty years ago, but we still talk sometimes four to five times a year.

Another out-of-the-blue day arrived. I don't know what was happening in her life, but she went off about school days and how I didn't want her to have Icing, and her million-dollar friends—that was how she rolled—on and on and on. But what got me was that I wasn't about anything. Momoa (grandmother) always told me, "You can count your friends on one hand. If you're lucky, Monkey, you may have lots of acquaintances but not friends."

Now you know, little Miss Brilliant thought she didn't know what she was talking about. *Stunned* wasn't the word. *Flabbergasted* won't even work. After this friend went on with her madwoman rave, can you believe I had no comeback for her? I want to tell you God had changed me, but that would be a lie. I've come to a point in my life that no matter what you do or say to hurt someone, God's going to fix it. When I moved again, I didn't give my telephone number out.

She kept going by to an aunt's house, giving her telephone number since she had also moved, and told her to call me. She needed me to come and see about her. Now mind you, she has a mom, sisters, and brothers in town. When I told my aunt what happened, I did say I was not angry, and to this day, I'm still not. I did pray she gets well.

Twelve years with me not returning calls, I still do have her number. She called another cousin trying to reach me, and she inadvertently gave her my number. She called, claiming we were family and bragging about how well everything was. Never did I hear, not once—thank You, Jesus—of what she accomplished. Hook, line, and sinker, she brought up Cookie, flaunting how she knew I wish my mother was living so I could take her on international endeavors as she does with her mom. Satan was still busy, but I had an answer for him. Let me tell you, that flamethrower was under my bed, but I promise not to use it. I don't want to have to use this weapon. To this day, I still love her. Take care, my millionaire friend.

CHAPTER 14

Icing on the Cake—Coveted

I finally got Icing, or so I thought. No, I wasn't diabetic then, but it may have led me to become one. This was all I ever imagined in my life to make me happy. Being the grown-up version of little Miss Brilliant, I should have known something by now. All I knew was that this was the answer to every problem in my life. This man was smart, the polar opposite of Suit.

When people go through rough marriages and life experiences, you'd think a change comes. But it doesn't, not until you really find God. Suit was good at trying to tear you down with stories about this woman or that woman, but he wasn't as bad as this man. I had known him since the seventh grade, but I didn't really know him, and when I got to know him, it wasn't what I thought. I tried telling myself a lot of things I knew weren't true, to make myself feel better. With Suit, I knew, but I should have known better when I found out he was married and the stunt about seeing me. God gave me the insight to flee at a young age. I hightailed it back to California so life could go on, and I did listen.

Nine hundred years passed, and whoa, it was me. This whatever it was came back to seek, search, and destroy, and it succeeded. Like I said, where was the whiff when I needed it? Be careful what you wish for, but the trick is that it has to wish for you; otherwise, you never get it. Or it's not what you wanted at all. Just keep on living. Momoa was still present and with me.

I couldn't believe any person could do the things emotionally that he did, and I thought Suit was the worst thing in the world.

See, little Miss Brilliant must have some serious issues. What in the world? I'd psych myself out and be in denial with things like, "He's not married to me, it doesn't matter." I had an excuse for all the verbal drama to make myself feel better. Did it work? No!

I got just what I deserved, probably more, and now I thought I got even more. But can you believe it shaped me into the person I am today? Whoever said sticks and stones may break your bones, but words will never hurt you? I beg to differ. When you're carrying a flamethrower, it will do more than hurt you.

Words broke me in half. I would have preferred the sticks and stones. The talk I heard kept playing in my head over and over again, and it wasn't anything that God had said. So wait a minute, who was this impersonating our Father, talking to me like they were judge and jury, my creator, trying to make me feel like the scum of the earth? I decided this must be "reaping what you sow."

I didn't do well in home economics in school. A gym bag, trying to get it right, almost killed me. The teacher kept making me redo an invisible zipper. Now what person can cut out a pattern right (cut darts and all) and thought she could master this class? No! This motto of stop reaping, so I quit sewing, along with stop reaping. I decided I'd come out of the land of dry bones to the place where I'd been broken, and I mean every bone destroyed. My journey paralleled that of Ezekiel 37:1–10, a passage that had become a metaphor for my life. Coming out of there, I witnessed transformation as God put me back together and the healing began. "Onward, Christian Soldier" now resonated over and over in my head, and oh, by the way, what good is Icing with no cake (lol)? Enjoy your endeavors.

CHAPTER 15

A Friend to the End

My all-around and through-it-all friend, you know I mentioned when I latch onto friends, they become family. Even the ones after harm was done remained just distant family members. I was once told I should bury the hatchet but leave the handle sticking out. When you know better and realize an individual doesn't stop, you should know where it is. It's like looking for that favorite red shoe; knowing where it is on a special occasion, not running around trying to find it, looking high and low. It's in there with the green ones. Get yourself organized, and you can get dressed faster.

The team of Frick and Frack was unstoppable until I began to wonder what makes people do what they do and call themselves friends or tell you they love you. I guess that's what we say about loving the Lord and doing any and everything to disprove that we do, each and every day. When people tell you the same things about the company you keep, remember what Momoa said: everybody can't be wrong. I'm the person who, no matter what happens elsewhere, gives you a chance. Exceptions can be made, sometimes. We err; it's only human, but being detrimental is not okay.

On this forever friendship where you'll defend until the end (gossip, rumors), I now see but over a forty-seven-year span. Yeah, this insane person really kept turning the other cheek. We met when she gave me a ride home one night. Like I said, I give credit where credit is due. Pregnant with baby number two, she was a nice person (still is), but the straight path traveled somehow turned a little crooked. When returning back to work, I went to a different location for a while. So when an opening came up in my original area, closer to home, I came back, and our friendship resumed.

We confided in all things: the good, bad, and ugly. Remember, we had some of the same relatives in the country, so that really made us family. Through the divorce and all, she was right there. She had her crying moments, me too. Enough of those, as they say, "cry me a river." Well, we had oceans of it. Pity parties are awful. After you get it all out, you feel better until the next time, and there is always a next time. If it was not for her, then me, and on and on. Once I fell short on a bill until payday, I tried to borrow money from her, and her reply was, "I'm not a bank." Well, you can't get mad about it because that's how I learned about an extension. Good for me. It's okay.

I got in an automobile accident and couldn't work for a while. My main job gave me disability payments, but the part-time job did not. Oh Lord, it really got tough, and trust me, I wouldn't ask again. That Christmas, my musketeers didn't get anything except what Cookie (Mama) could get from a charity organization (fruit, candy, and little trinkets kind of toys), but that's not how our Christmas usually was. Toys galore, clothes—whatever they wanted they got. That Christmas really taught me about being humble. People always said I spoiled my kids rotten, but it wasn't like that. I just had to be both parents, and that's what I did and always have.

My baby, Brilliant, was so tiny. She'd make clothes for herself, giving credit where credit is due. Sometimes I'd charge something at my part-time job on her account using discounts for me and her, like I said, family.

I was so heartbroken about Christmas. You know, we had a Christmas we never forgot in January of the next year. My settlement came through. I could afford to buy us a house. I still worked the two jobs, but that's okay too. Rumors where I worked were always going around and usually were true. Three months after I'd asked a supervisor about it, she said not to her knowledge. We were always in the news, but I wouldn't have bought the house knowing we were in jeopardy like that. Well, you know me, things happen. Around this time, I was asking God to send me someone. I would have been praying for this job not to shut down. I had been there for nineteen years and needed eleven more for my thirty years.

The day the boom fell, I was at my part-time job, and my boss came in and asked me what I knew. I confidently said the rumors about the closing weren't true, and he said, "Let's go look at the TV." At that moment, I really thought I was going to have a nervous breakdown right then. I couldn't believe this, especially when the 411 got all the info, information that I apparently lacked. I was scheduled to be at work by 1:30 p.m. and managed to go downtown to our building. In front of the building, the guard had to help me get in. The news teams had taken over the entrance and exits. I was trying to hold it together. The TV news team was no stranger, but this was my career, not some tour of the building and how things work.

When I got off the elevator, since I was the last to come in until 3:00 p.m., all the big wigs were there, and even my supervisor was crying. We'd heard other places were closing but rest assured, not the teams that were always leading the nation. I have to admit we were superb. With accommodations galore, we were the epitome of excellence, because that's what we stood for, and yet there we were, facing shutdown. Oh yeah, if your record was good, you had the option to transfer, but a lot of people were in for a rude awakening. Thank God, I wasn't one of them.

By July of this year, Cookie (Mama) had passed, and I surely missed her. I knew I had to go somewhere, though I didn't know when or where, but it was coming. Yes, I continued working my part-time job until my papers confirmed my choice was approved, and I chose my husband's hometown. I was going to finally meet the new family; remember, I still had musketeers and two out of three in high school by then.

On this journey, the team remained together even after the statement about Cookie's passing. Well, I knew she was going to die. Do you remember the whiff earlier in my days when I shared this info about childhood with her? She threw that up, but we were still a team. You see, I had turned the other cheek.

As we traveled to the new location, the deal was that we would split the rental car and expenses because we had a free place to stay with my new mother-in-law, which was a relief. So it was basically just gas. Her relocation didn't arrive at her home; that threw a wrench in things, so there I went, having her back. The relocation did arrive at my mother-in-law's home but not before we got there. Out of love, we paid your deposit and first month's rent; that's what true friends do, no pat on the back is needed or required. We found a place in the same complex. When we got back to move, we never mentioned gas, rental, or anything. It was okay.

Regarding the packing, I had lots of furniture, so I needed the biggest U-Haul. She said she had hers covered. I called home; yes, I was still working full-time, but I had lots of help. Three men and a baby genius, who was now a teenage baby, were there. When the teenage baby answered and I asked how it was going, she said, "Mama, you're going to be…," and I just knew something was broken. She said they were over at the other team member's, packing her stuff on my truck. What? I wasn't brilliant at packing, but now I'm a pro. However, I had enough sense to know that wouldn't work. She didn't have much, but I did. You would think my packing men—husband, two sons, and a neighbor's son, whom I have known from birth like one of mine—would call your mother and tell her what was happening, or she could have called or something. By the time I got to her house, the truck was locked and ready to go. It was okay.

We arrived at the new location, and my TVs, dining table, and chairs were ruined. It was okay. This turning the other cheek was really wearing thin. Since we moved ourselves, you know the disaster was on me. The selling of my house was not profitable, but God made a way through another coworker whose brother was transferring to our town. The company I worked for paid all the fees for me, and they moved in and took over the note at that time, an assumption loan. So you see, it was okay—a blessing.

I had already established an account with the bank on our first trip there, but when her relocation came, she had to wait to pay me back. Sure. After the check cleared, you now say, "Can you pay me some of the money?" I wasn't rich back then, and I'm not rich now. I don't have it like that, so I need my money as I loaned it.

Then a personal story unfolded, dating all the way back to Christmas. My musketeers could only give what Grandmother (Cookie) could muster up. She explained this, that, and the other, but I didn't ask for anything. However, when she told me who and how much she'd given to someone else, I was shocked. I couldn't get $69.38 for two days from her, and yet she did this for someone else. Tell me, how did I rank so low in her book? It's okay, or was it?

We joined a church there. She met someone, but they didn't think married and single women should associate together. I had known her for at least seventeen years by then. Family, right? She obliged him. How much running together had I done? I've got kids, and one was really sick now. It seemed like the move made her worse; she'd undergone surgeries and transfusions which she'd never had. Now she had a stroke. So how much were we running together? Back home, I had a mother's life. She's the single one. Not to make fun, but was I too busy working and trying to care for my musketeers?

She married him and once mentioned a dinner at their home, exclusively for Christians. We all attend the same church, yet I guess I wasn't invited. It hurt, but was it really okay? Before her marriage, our complex transitioned to low-income housing, and we received another notice. I loaned her money, expecting repayment from her rapid refund tax. I always came to her aid. When tax season arrived, I was there with her. Despite hearing about her wedding and other things, all I needed was my money back—I had bills to pay too. Then came an overtime opportunity at work: twelve hours a day, four days a week. I seized every hour I could, while she didn't have to, given her situation. For me and mine, it was a blessing. Baby Genius was frequently hospitalized. I didn't mind being with her. Even my FMLA leave was used for her, not for myself.

On the day we moved in, there was black ice on the ground. The moment my husband warned, "Look out," it was too late. I slipped, landing hard and fracturing my tailbone. Before I could even adjust to the new office, while preparing for the hospital, Baby Genius suffered her first stroke, at least the first I was aware of. X-rays showed the extent of damage to her brain over the years. Now she was sixteen and in a dire state, which meant traction was out of the question for me—I would be living at the children's hospital. So you see, I'm grappling with serious issues, but hey, I learned about black ice, something I'd never heard of or seen before.

So you see, those twelve-hour days and the constant need for overtime were blessings because all I did was sit, talk, and listen. That tailbone did what it needed to do on its own, but it never really healed properly. Nevertheless, I was as good as could be and grateful.

Her new marriage changed her. She moved further away, ending our ride-sharing arrangement. Four years passed, and another boom was on the way. My musketeers had all grown up, so when my chance came, I seized it, relocating just 150 miles from where they remained. Baby Genius didn't want to come. I wished she had, but I couldn't keep her in diapers forever. I still tried, and now she was twenty years old. Yeah, yeah, yeah, right, right, right.

Really, I experienced two booms simultaneously. The first was the closing, but with the second, I went back to talk to the relocation manager, a genuinely nice person. I hadn't had many dealings with her or her team, but whenever she spoke about them, she seemed pleasant. When she called me into her office and properly introduced herself, asking about where in my home state my family was originally from, who my people were, and just having a friendly chat, I found myself wishing she had been my manager. But oh well. When I told her about Cookie (Mama) and the little hick country town of my people, she exclaimed, "I can't believe it. I'm from a town about eleven miles from there."

As we kept talking and I mentioned Mama's name, she was astonished. She inquired about my grandmother's, aunts', and uncles' names. Then she said, "I'm going to make a phone call." I thought the call was about rumors of a town opening up thirty minutes away, where I was planning to go back home. But that wasn't it.

An elderly lady was on the phone, and she said, "Mama, you're not going to believe who I'm sitting here with." When she revealed I was talking to Momoa's oldest sister, whom I only knew by one name, I was at a loss for words. "What!" We chatted for at least forty-five minutes, and she had to be family because she knew everyone's nicknames, which even I had. It's funny when you have to ask about a person's given name. I'd been there four years and had my own family right under my nose. I had plenty of coworkers, but I mostly kept to myself. I've learned some, not completely where I should be; that comes later, but I still felt a bit out of whack.

Now for the second boom. When she started talking about people and whom to trust, I listened intently. She was older, not as old as Cookie (Mama) and my aunts, but she knew a lot. When she said, "The team is not your friend," I was shocked. Does "what?" have to be in my constant vocabulary? It seems so.

This new cousin told me things that no one else in the office would. Not just personal gossip, but all my flaws, no compliments, just trash talk about my family and all. You always think you've heard it all until the next revelation. When I left her office, being the next relocation, she had time to chat. She was telling other office managers how we were related, and yes, when she took time off for a funeral at home, it was for my mama Cookie. She regretted not questioning me when I arrived, and everyone was shocked. It's a small world.

When my time came to leave, she was curious about the commotion upfront. She noted, "It took longer for you than for any other relocation to sign and come out of the office." What was she talking about? I simply said nothing. I didn't dare say, but what made me proud was perhaps my new cousin wanted to know if I was as bad about spilling secrets as she was. You know, if I had exposed her secrets, my cousin would have said, "She's as bad as the team. They're meant for each other, two of a kind." But I would never do that. Sure, rumors swirled about her, but saints are down here. That's my motto. I left her there and went on to my next relocation, she stayed put, and then came another relocation two years later, followed by the final lap of my journey.

Things were different for me and the team. They had returned home and entered different fields of work. When I retired—thank You, Lord—I had completed thirty-one years and six months of service. I wanted to show that God is good, even when we don't deserve it. Indeed, I had exhibited plenty of bad behaviors, which I left behind before my second relocation.

When her mother passed away, she called me, and both my husband and I went over, despite her apparent lack of care for me. She was visibly upset, and out of my mouth came the words, "Well, you knew she was going to die." I'm still surprised God didn't snatch me up right then. Her husband and mine both gave me stern looks.

Her husband objected, "You don't talk to my wife like that."

I retorted, "That's what she said to me when my Mama Cookie died."

They both looked as guilty as the proverbial cat that ate the rat. I won't lie, it felt good. I was sick and tired of people speaking to me disrespectfully. Not that day.

When we left her house, my husband expressed his disbelief: "I can't believe she did you like that after all you did for her when we moved." I had attended her mother's funeral, and this lady had been as good as gold. Her entire family treated me like a sister, and her mother always remembered to bake me a coconut cake on my birthday. Rest in peace and thank you.

After retiring, I considered returning to her field of work. She had said, "What I do, you need experience." I had none, but someone had trained her. At our last job, you couldn't just walk in off the street and start working.

During a visit back home, I went to her office, which seemed like a fantastic job with little public interaction—my idea of heaven. Surprisingly, her boss showed up, introduced herself, and asked when I would join her team. She'd heard good things about me, but I confessed I lacked experience for the job. She challenged, "Who told you that? You don't need any." I admitted I didn't know where I got that idea.

Someone else had merely asked, "When are you going to learn?"

Yet, I still wasn't ready for a change.

On my last visit home, I had to leave earlier than planned and called her. She had remarried and hadn't mentioned that her stepkids visited on Saturdays, and they attended church together on Sundays. Had I known I was imposing—I didn't think so, as she had visited me—I wouldn't have asked to stay. I still had other relatives—aunts and cousins—but I requested just one overnight stay. It turned out to be an imposition, as I spent the whole night sitting in a chair. When she said, "I don't know what to tell you," that was my breaking point. She drove me to the airport, and that's when I truly learned to be true to myself. All the excuses and denials I clung to vanished on that flight. I realized I had turned the other cheek enough.

Despite everything, I reminded myself it wasn't that bad. I hadn't been crucified; I didn't have to sacrifice my life for humanity. And as the saying goes, "Jesus loves me. This I know," so what did I have to complain about? Life is meant to be lived, and though I could recount endless stories, why should I? I've encountered emotional turmoil, but it's nothing I can't survive from. Hope isn't lost, as I'm just passing through on my way home. Life might toss you into stormy seas, with winds howling and fires raging, but try not to be the cause of it all.

Prayer has been and continues to be my solace. Without it, I don't know where I'd be. The first time I was called upon to pray aloud in church was a transformative moment. Initially, fear gripped me, but then the internal storm calmed, the raging fire within me was stilled, and I have been in that peaceful state since. I know Big Mama, Momoa, and yes, Cookie (Mama) would be proud.

CHAPTER 16

Perhaps If

Perhaps if I had told you of my heartache, you would have done something, the answer would be this: it didn't change things. Perhaps if I had reminded you that I thought you were my BFF (best friend for life, it didn't matter. Perhaps if I'd said, "Rumor has it. What's your truth?" you'd deny it. Perhaps if I had just known that down the road, terrible things happen among friends, the answer would be this: it didn't help. Perhaps I'd just take the blame for everything, not judge you, understand how you could do these things when earlier signs were there, stop suffocating you with caring and concern, giving you when I had none to give, begging, pleading, and becoming a throwaway person when the whole world turned its back on you, taking a bullet for you and not hesitating to do so, and just giving you my all and all, but, most of all, loving you when I didn't love myself because you were my life. The answer: it didn't make a difference. Learn to give yourself!

CHAPTER 17

The Pathfinder

Don't let this life be about you. Don't try to be Christ; that title has already been claimed and given. Being Christlike is your goal. Jesus had problems while He walked this earth, to show people what can happen even though you've done nothing but try to save them. He was already heaven-bound but came down so we would be too. Now tell me, isn't that a fantastic dream that came true? I need you, not want you, to stay focused and pray for one another, no matter what. There was a time when I couldn't do that. I saw myself on murderous shows as the villain, not the victim, and thought revenge was the ultimate goal. Why not? An eye for an eye and all that goes with it. Can you believe I convinced myself that the book of Ecclesiastes 3:1-11 was written just for me?

The Time

It came, and I almost lost my soul. Indeed, I had wanted to seek revenge on those who had torn me apart, made me cry, and hurt my children. I say *my children* because irresponsibility led to their being discarded like trash. I do understand when a couple doesn't want to be together, but the children remain a part of the picture, whether one likes it or not. How could a Christian feel this way? I found myself capable of being an ambulance murderess. If I were to go to prison, my first thought was that my children would have no one to care for them. No amount of anger could justify subjecting them to more abuse than they had already endured.

On another note, I must admit, no more shopping and shopping channels, no doing as I pleased, no more hair salons, sodas whenever I liked, just freedom. I could repent all day, every day, but I'd still be locked up. Was killing someone, regardless of what they did or said, worth it? They weren't that important, yet I still felt bad. I couldn't forgive myself, so I believed I hadn't repented enough. I kept being miserable and denying it. This sounded like madness to me, and then it struck me: they probably weren't feeling my pain and despair. At first, I desperately wanted them to. But would I truly feel better deep down? No, but we tell ourselves, "It's all about me, my suffering, how I deserved better treatment."

I considered myself a good person (to an extent) but never as bad as they were. I felt like an avenging angel. Yes, I had earned that title. Understanding my people and where I come from, it took me a while to say, "Stop!" These wrongdoers weren't going to get away with what they had done. Somehow, some way they're going to pay. Sitting in church, yes, in church, such malice ran rampant within me. I believed in God and never ceased, but this feeling of needing justice wouldn't go away.

Being remarried for at least twenty-three years at that time, I still had certain thoughts on my mind until I was in church. Many of us are in church, dressed impeccably, yet our minds are elsewhere— thinking of malls, ballgames, fishing trips, vacations, and everything imaginable.

On this particular Sunday, the bishop said, "If you don't learn to forgive, you're going to end up in hell." What? It was at that precise moment I realized I hadn't truly forgiven many people, although I thought I had. The things done to my children were a significant part of my inability to forgive. He said, "God forgives you, no matter what when you ask for forgiveness. He does, so shouldn't you also forgive?" When I looked up, he seemed to be looking directly at me, or so I thought. Guilt can make you see many things, and that day I did. Who had ordained me to be the avenging angel?

"Revenge is Mine," said the Lord, and trust me, it is. So you see, this too passed, and thank You, Jesus, that it did. They didn't steal my thunder; I knew my worth. Looking back over my life, can you believe I'm grateful? How else could I have learned what some people are really like, the do's and don'ts—that's why it's called life. I remember Momoa (grandmother) saying, "I had to laugh to keep from crying." Me too, Momoa, me too.

So don't beat yourself up. I feel like they missed out; my blessings still flow. Trouble doesn't last always. Leave the past in the past. Never try to return. Don't dwell on what-ifs, try a different dessert—leave the icing on the cake, try a bowl of fruit instead. You see, when you learn to forgive, you'll feel so much better.

Now that soda is a different story. Feeding it with a long-handled spoon won't work; just don't feed it at all.

How did God show me? Look around—I still love you in spite of everything, I've forgiven you, so you can surely forgive yourself. It's time. I want you to follow the path to Philippians 4:11: "Be content in whatever state you find yourself." I've gone to the cross for you. My love is evident because I will be with you forever. The blessings we receive that flow from day to day, even when we fall short, still abound. His mercy endureth forever, so raise that glass of soda, etc., to the high heavens. Cheers! I stay on the path, the pathfinder.

CHAPTER 18

The Altar Call

My church has always had a period for altar calls, and no matter how many times I relocated—a total of three—every place I worshiped did the same. My journey with altar calls began in my hometown as an adult. I witnessed many people respond, but I always stayed in my seat. I did kneel and pray, but was I truly sincere? Yes, I talked to God, but at that time, I thought I was being sincere, yet apparently, I wasn't fully aware of my insincerity. Sin is sin, no matter how you dress it up, whether you drive it to town, or go to church in your finest clothes, and all the other places you visit. I had thought altar calls were strictly for church, but I realized you must practice what you preach.

Now you might be thinking, *She's got that flamethrower under the bed*, but bear with me, I'm getting there. Exactly three years to the day after my mother Cookie passed away (April 8, 1988), I met the man I am now married to. On Sunday, April 6, 1991, I went to the altar call, not just kneeling at my seat but actually responding to the call. I asked God to send me someone who would love me and my three kids. I had enough of blind dates that left me *blind* and not-so-blind dates with people I thought I knew. I met Jekylls and Hydes, bigamists, you name it, I encountered it. You know when you've had enough, and my cup was overflowing. My youngest daughter even decided she was going to find herself a dad. She picked a policeman, and that situation went way off the rails. You know how they say women like men in uniforms; I guess even I fell for a couple of them, not sure whom they were serving and protecting—oh yes, themselves.

I've always requested the day off from work on the anniversary of Cookie's (my mother's) death. It's been thirty-five years in 2023, and it's still hard for me. I stopped going to church on Mother's Day, but in the past few years, I've gotten better. It still rocks my soul, but I know Mary's baby is around. All I have to do is call Him. I want to remember that word: *call.* This particular year, I didn't get April 8 off, and I was upset. Who wants a Tuesday off unless it's for a significant reason? We could trade days off at work if we found someone to swap with, but I found no one. I started to consider calling out, but maybe it's time to face this issue. You can't feel this way forever, or can you?

I went to work in a bad mood, and we all had our tricks of the trade. We learned to stay a minute or two later than our assigned break time so we could sit together. For instance, if she got out at one thirty, we'd stay until one thirty-one, and by then whoever was coming in would take your card. By one thirty-two, everyone was in position. Trust me, we figured out how to make this work. So I figured I'd take my best friend because she didn't put her card up until everyone was seated. I took her turn when she came back into our pod, and the next person did the same. That's how we all did it in our pod, and yes, everybody else was doing the same. We were all happy.

That day, exactly three years later, everyone remembered and was surprised to see me, but my other half (we were a duo called Frick and Frack) knew I was working. Coming from my other job, which I loved, I plugged in, and a call was coming in. It was like I couldn't even catch my breath, but you know, the board was smart enough that it should never show the count of being off. We had to have ourselves together to pull off our tricks without being detected. I always wondered if the management ever figured it out. Everything was really technical with a head count, signals by time of day, and peak and off-peak. It was no joke, but like I said, where there's a will, there's a way, and we found a way.

Little did I know that what I prayed for was coming in on the line. This was a workplace, not a dating service. I had never done anything but take requests, but this man just kept on and on, like he does today, telling me some things about himself while I processed what he needed to be done. Marital status, job, looking for a wife—what? Now mind you, I did not ask Mary's baby for a husband. Or did I? You know, I am a product of Mary's baby. I love calling Jesus that. Momoa (grandmother) used to say that all the time; there was just something about hearing that. You know, after the altar call, I felt like He was all mine. Don't say it, I know—little Miss Brilliant still has issues of selfishness but then I learned that no matter where you are, you can have that feeling. Just meditate where you please, and I mean anywhere. I have to do that a lot and I love it.

The location of my now-husband was Milton, Florida. He told me he had just finished praying for a wife. Well, that was the first time I'd heard that line. Who was he trying to fool? Nope. What made me give out my telephone number, I don't know, but I unintentionally gave out the wrong one. Honestly, he was going to call. Did he know? When Frick called, I said he was a liar, as usual. Little did I know until the next day that this young man had called all night long until he found someone in my unit. At that time, there were so many units all over the US; reaching me or my unit again could only be an act of God.

My coworker said the phone number I gave him was wrong. She left me a personal note on the message board. Looking at my phone number, I kept saying this was my number, but I had transposed the last two digits. He left me a number to call and speak to his mother to give him the correct number. What? So I did leave a message on her machine but noticed it was a young woman's voice. Can you believe I left such a foul message because he said he wasn't married? Caught in a lie already. I know a young female's voice from an old woman's, and yes, I told her all about her "husband" and that he was out there riding the road and picking up women from one state to another. They say truckers aren't any good, and he was one of them. Yeah! Give him my number so I can tell him to his face what I think of him. How could she be married to such a man? Yeah, I went off so badly that I had to call back to finish what I had to say. Take that, Mr. Trucker.

Well, the musketeers and I were eating dinner together, which was a rare occasion. Baby Genius answered the phone, and she said a lady was asking for me. I got to the phone, and she asked if I was who I was, so I said yes. I knew she couldn't be a teacher, so I figured maybe the church. Nope, it was his mother, explaining that the voice I heard was his sister's (RIP). She said he wasn't married, all the things I would later find out to be true. She did say that she and her sister had never laughed so much in all their lives when they heard my messages. Now what could I say? Oh yes, I had to apologize, and even say I know my mama (Cookie) and grandmother turned over in their graves. I wasn't brought up like that and expressed deep regret. I almost couldn't stop. I felt justified at the time of my rant and rave, but even being insane was put to shame. That excuse just wouldn't fly.

That lady became my mother-in-law in three months. Yes, three months, and as I said, thirty-two years in 2023, we remain. I didn't say it was all smooth sailing because I do know I'm a force to be reckoned with. I know that young man learned about prayer if he didn't know how before. I have to rein myself in a lot, but now I know how.

Our Father, who art in heaven, hallowed be Thy name; Thy kingdom come; Thy will be done; on earth as it is in heaven. Give us this day our daily bread. And forgive us our trespasses, as we forgive those who trespass against us. And lead us not into temptation, but deliver us from evil. For Thine is the kingdom, the power, and the glory forever. Amen!

CHAPTER 19

Know It, Love It, Embrace It

I wanted this for you to know of our Savior Jesus Christ. I knew that in this life, trouble wouldn't last always; it couldn't because our God was always on duty. Never seeing it coming was not an option because we were forewarned. God had a plan for each and every one of us. I knew it!

Do not try to change God's plan. He would do that for you. The change was already done, so all that was required was you. There were so many prayers and sayings in place; use them, meditate on them. Love it, God's creation!

Stay in the light, the door is not locked. Nightmares came in the day as well as the darkness. I was in the dark for so long because of how the people in the world treated me, but God treated me so much better. He became the "know it, love it, and embrace it." Take that, Satan.

CHAPTER 20

Sharing My Wishlist

You know, when you share your wish list with others, sometimes they try to fulfill what's on it as a gift. So here goes mine:

1. My foremost wish is for you to know, trust, and believe in God. If only one item on my list is to be fulfilled, let this be it.
2. A life free from heartache and struggle.
3. I wish my three musketeers had been born to two loving parents, not just one, and grew in Christ as they were taught.
4. I wish I had made only the right choices in life. While my wrongdoings caused pain and suffering, they taught me valuable lessons. Thankfully, God has forgiven me. Wish granted!
5. I wish this book reaches someone who has seen worse than me. Not everything was revealed here, but I've received a revelation from God for my soul. Wish granted!
6. My wish extends to everyone—friends, foes, loved ones, those yet to enter or leave my life, and those on the fence. May we all learn from life's experiences that we are not alone.

We must remember that God sent Jesus in human form to assure us of His presence until the end. Wish granted!

I wish for us to avoid seeking revenge. Instead, we should do things we'll be proud to remember, not those we'd rather forget. Deep transgressions take time to heal. I hope the desire for revenge fades away; it's costly and can lead to the loss of one's soul.

With these wishes fulfilled, I believe we can all enter heaven. Fulfilled. Amen.

CHAPTER 21

Just-Once List

There are all kinds of *just-once* situations, and I know I have an addictive nature, so the concept of *just once* is a rarity. The things we tell ourselves or the things we wish to have or try just once. Right, there is letting us know whatever endeavor it is, it usually signifies a transgression. The *just-once* factor was saying, "I can stop," when we know it's just the beginning. The yearning or the lure of pretense is setting us up for failure. How many *just-once* situations have you tried? Before going to the *just-once* prayer, it might have needed to intervene so that "just once" wouldn't happen, but if you must try "just once," please try God!

Redeemed!

CHAPTER 22

Grace Is Sweet

You needed to and should have lived life under God's umbrella. I couldn't say you wouldn't get wet, but you would stay dry. The rain and winds blew, it got dark, you fell, got bumps and bruises everywhere, sometimes even broken bones, including internal organs like a broken heart that wouldn't mend. But when you started confessing to Christ, the first questions usually asked were, "Why me? Why not you?"

In the soul, we had committed so many sins, and the worst ones were committed when we knew beforehand it was wrong. We concocted excuses, and yes, I'm writing about what I personally knew. We wanted Grace and Mercy due to being ashamed of ourselves until the next time. When you repented and no longer ventured down sin lane, grace took over because you saw you could no longer drive on this lane or Destruction Avenue. Grace and Mercy took over.

Just ask.

CHAPTER 23

The Bitter Pill

A medical checkup is required here to get the spiritual checkup. We may walk around suited up dolled up, made up immaculately, pristine, and not a hair out of place, but are you really dressed? On the outside you are; you never know what's going on, on the inside. Externally, we may seem the epitome of health, but it's what's inside that counts. The stories our insides could tell, of the bitter pills we've swallowed, perhaps even overdosed on. While it was working, the side effects are ugly sores that spread throughout our system; hatred and malice flow to the bloodstream, taking control of the brain, and making us think, "I want to be turned up or turned out." It took hold of being turned on to God, so if by mistake you swallowed the pill, wash it down with prayer; there's still time to do so, but *hurry*!

The doctor of the soul is called the Savior.

CHAPTER 24

Meeting the Soul Slayer— Confessions

I hesitated to tell you this, but I know you'll wonder, so I'll be honest. I've been to very low places in my life. Yes, I'll just say it, suicide crossed my mind after Cookie gained her wings and flew away. I felt utterly alone, and the depth of that loneliness became clearer later. I consider myself strong, but there's a limit to what one can endure. Yet I remind myself they didn't crucify me, so it can't be that bad.

God gave me life, not to take it away. The ticket to His kingdom is His gift, so why squander it? I hold the key to enter. Here, my three beloved children whom I love dearly came into the picture.

Being a sole parent is like two full-time jobs, stretching me thin, but love stretched me even further. Who would they have if I left? I couldn't bear leaving them alone, though the long hours I worked felt like a different kind of suicide. The thought of enduring eternal torment, when I already felt like I was living in hell here, was unbearable. My three musketeers, in a way, saved me. I struggled to show them that they were loved and not alone, just as they struggled with Cookie's departure. I couldn't let the soul slayer win.

Time will slay you. As Momoa said, "Just keep on living," and that's what I did, not by my own strength alone. I wondered if mental illness was taking over me, with intrusive thoughts creeping in. But prayer and clinging to Jesus kept me grounded. He loved me and was teaching me lessons I needed to learn to endure the future. And endure I did. I'm still standing!

The pain of living is different from the pain of death. A simple "Thank You, Jesus" seems insufficient for surviving. Day-to-day pain leads to hope, wisdom, knowledge, and mercy, teaching you how to face obstacles and make the right choices. Hope springs eternal with the promise of heaven.

If I can prevent even one person from taking their life, I'll have succeeded. You can't truly help someone unless you've been there in thought yourself. I now know that suicide wasn't the answer regardless of the circumstances. That soul slayer, as tempting as it was, met its match.

Remember, when you go to God in prayer, and it must be sincere, accept His answer even if it's not what you wanted. That's how you keep the soul slayer at bay. It tries to sneak in, not bold enough to confront you directly. The real world does not allow you to sleep when the soul slayer is around; send it in God's way, and trust me, it will eventually flee. Don't let it stop you from reaching the kingdom.

Game on, soul slayer.

I've already won.

CHAPTER 25

Whom I Call On

Since becoming an adult, I've realized I might not reach the genius level. That status seems unattainable to me, as you can see. I've come to accept that one can't possibly know everything, even though some people think they do.

I've often contemplated the idea of sharing God. For a while, I wanted to hoard Him all to myself, like my affection for Momoa. When I truly understood His power and who He is (which some still don't grasp), I was tempted to keep Him like a penny in my pocket, always there for me. But then I thought about others who are lost and in need, so I decided to share Him with you.

God is necessary for the things I've faced and will face. Somewhere, someone is crying for many reasons—grief, a broken heart, a sick loved one, feeling lost, needing healing for body and soul, lacking trust, hope, or faith, or praying for someone who won't pray for themselves, especially those who haven't come to Christ. Our souls are doomed, and that's really not where you want anyone to be. I know our souls are important. We often treat each other as if we're not, saying and doing the wrong things. But there is nothing our God can't fix. Just because it may not be fixed the way you want, doesn't mean it's not being addressed.

God's goodness is so immense that you might want to keep Him all to yourself, but I'll gladly share Him. In fact, I must share Him. You must try Him because, believe it or not, He's been there for you, hearing you, wiping your tears, opening your eyes, and pouring out blessings you haven't deserved, even without a thank-you from you. I share Him out of love, wanting you to know Jesus Christ, Mary's baby, the promise keeper, prayer receiver and answerer, source of joy, faith, hope, and love, savior, comforter, redeemer, bread when hungry, and rock in a weary land. You'll discover what you call Him, and He'll be many things to you, as He is to me. We should not be empty wells because our cups run over with Christ in our lives.

I sometimes want to say "my God," but I've learned to share Him with you. Amen.

CHAPTER 26

You Becoming the Change

Never think I claim to be all holy; that's not the essence of this book. I still need to call upon the Lord constantly to keep my inner flamethrower, my avenging angel, in check. The difference now is that I remember to call on Him, unlike before when I thought I knew my purpose and mission without His guidance. I was so sure I was right, and guilt didn't enter the picture, which says a lot.

You might think I knew everything, but I was far from it. I wasn't listening to God because if I had, I would have heard His Words. I walked around acting like an avenging angel, thinking I was righteous, but I was more like someone with a pitchfork instead of wings. That's not the kind of mission God sends His angels on.

I once had a personal license plate labeled "the 411." I thought I had all the information or knew where to find it. My job required listening and being knowledgeable, patient, and understanding what was needed in each situation. You must listen; don't always be the one talking. I could do all that, but did I seek guidance through prayer or the Bible? No, I just resorted to flamethrowing and pitchforking.

If you're waiting for others to change, stop! Change begins with you. Always start with yourself. Who do you know better? Make a difference; big or small, it counts. Hardships happen to everyone. Looking back, I know I can't and don't want to let my past life return. You must learn from your mistakes and fix them internally. Don't expect from others what you're not willing to do yourself.

This former avenging angel always had to have the last word in an argument at any cost. Now I've learned the true value of silence.

It has served me well, day and night. I remember Momoa's grandmother (now our grandmother, lol) used to say, "You'll argue with a signboard." I didn't know what she was talking about, with her dialect blending the words. But now I get it. As a kid, I didn't grasp it, but I'm stopping you from going south because, by now you love her too. So you see, little Miss Brilliant is working on this. Sometimes, my best response is no response at all. Once you've spoken, you can't take words back. I hate saying I'm sorry, so often, staying silent works best for me. You've probably noticed I still have a bit of that *brilliant* thing going on.

Words can be abusive, so be careful not to say the wrong ones, like Big Mama used to, especially when you know what you're doing. I've mastered most of my changes, but the flamethrower is still there, under the bed, just not loaded (semiretired).

CHAPTER 27

To Thine Own Self Be True

We don't always get what we want in life; instead, we receive what comes our way. As you delve into this book, you might find reflections of yourself and wonder by events that unfold, *Was this woman peeking into my life? Did she peek through my window, hide under my bed, or lurk in my closet, capturing my story?* Gazing into the mirror, you double-check your reality, pondering if you've stepped into the pages of this book.

I share these words because deep down, I believe someone else understands how someone tried to dim your light, extinguish your candle, or steal your thunder, shaking the very foundation of your being.

Yet God remains your unwavering light, your enduring candle, your resonant thunder. No matter the circumstances, He can relight many candles and calm the roaring thunders. God is your path forward, a testament to being a work in progress and a child of God.

CHAPTER 28

Sooner or Later

You had tried everything that didn't work: the diet, the new hair color and cut, a new wardrobe, just all kinds of physical changes. After all this self-improvement, all you can say is, "Well, something is still missing," like the cake you made—you missed an ingredient somewhere, took it out of the oven, and it fell flat. Well!

Now I'll tell you about failing to try the most important thing that will make all that success you're after. If you try Our Father, I mean really try, I guarantee all that you're trying to do will turn out better.

We all come His way, usually when in trouble, but He doesn't care how you get there; just get there, then you'll be able to hear Him say, "Servant, well done."

And remember, have you added a "cup of God" to your life's recipe? It makes everything rise and taste better.

CHAPTER 29

My Soul Finds Comfort

You may have searched high and low, and you may never know or understand how your life took this turn, but in life's lessons, there's a reason. You wouldn't be where you are at this very moment if you weren't meant to be. On Sunday mornings, you can find me doing the verbal prayer, and in the moment, I know that's where I am supposed to be, getting my soul comforted. I pray every day, and talking with God does me good. Oh yeah, it's not just once a day, but He never gets tired of me. Ask me how I know because my prayers are answered, and I've learned to accept the answer because I understand why, if it's not what I want to hear, it is always what I need to hear.

Sooner or later, through answered prayers, your soul, too, will find its comfort. Always!

CHAPTER 30

I Am the Work in Progress

I want to be able to tell you that I have arrived. Not so. The question is: Where do you wish to go? You can't arrive until you know where you are going. Destination? The real world will make you change your destination and purpose and deal with unforeseen bumps in the road.

Passages can lead to where you want to go, but was that your destination? A fork in the road can take you off course. The bump can land you softly or really hard. Your agenda is yours, not someone else's.

You do know there is a place just waiting, already prepared regardless of the bump, the fork, the detour, and any obstacle that might and will befall you. Trust me, that's all a part of the real world. In this course, the focus is to remember this is a temporary journey. If you wish your destination to be forever, I did tell you it's already straight ahead of you. Knot it in your heart and soul; believe it's yours. The kingdom is at hand; that's my destination. Each person must have their own. Just saying, I wish that becomes yours.

Passage for Me

At sixty-seven, this journey started. Little Miss Brilliant experienced a message, confirmation, dreams, and all kinds of things just for me to know from God. A lot of times, we don't act or understand, or being honest, don't want to when it's not pleasing to us.

All my signs came in less than a week. A young author was talking about her book being published. What? She is the only person that I've ever actually met in the flesh who has done this. We met at my church. She gave me permission to use her name, and so I will: Rosalind Smith. The nudge came from her. The dream in the real world is possible. No more procrastinating, it's not possible. Doubt went out the window.

A few days later, a message on my cell with my mom's name spelled correctly said, "Meet at 5:15." I didn't think that was funny in the least bit since my mom had been gone for thirty-five years. When I clicked the message, I found it to be dud; Baby Genius and I knew it wasn't her. I do have a cousin with that name, but I know she wouldn't do that.

I came out of the link because I knew something was wrong and found out she was not the sender of the message. Last but not least, my mom's favorite entertainer had a special on. This special had been on before, and I'd highlighted it when it came on again. Saw it from beginning to end. Her story was heartbreaking, but she's still around through it all and came out on top. This special, I know it wasn't just for me, but I felt that she was talking directly to me and for me. I knew God wanted me to help someone know He was here. That's not what she said—I repeat, that's not what she said, but that's what I felt and heard.

I saw in her that no matter what you go through and have to endure, you're not the only one, and most of all, you're not alone. The first time I heard "This too shall pass"—my first pastor always said that—I had no idea what that meant at the time, but trust me, I know now. I can't believe it even when I thought I was brilliant (at five to six years old) that went right over my head.

My intentions are pure and simple, not to bring tears because they do fall, but wherever you see, it's to let you know little Miss Brilliant had some comedy, trauma, drama, and a whole lot of chaos in her life, but I can laugh now that God got me through it, and I'm still here. So if you happen to pass me on the road somewhere and maybe see Matthew 6:9, you'll know God left little Miss Brilliant around on her travels.

I don't have the gift of voice like Cookie did. My gift came from paper and pen. I can reach the highest realms of the universe, I can reach a soul, and I can stay with you for a lifetime until the rapture comes. Words don't disappear nor are erased from memories; they linger and sometimes leave to make you whole when you've been cut into. Pen and paper is where we often return for solace, for the Bible has been around for ages. When you can't get it right, look there. Our Father is there, just waiting for you to unlock the door. Go ahead and turn the key. It was never locked in.

Our Father, who art in heaven, hallowed be Thy name; Thy kingdom come; Thy will be done, on earth as it is in heaven. Give us this day our daily bread. And forgive us our trespasses, as we forgive those who trespass against us. And lead us not into temptation, but deliver us from evil. For Thine is the kingdom, the power, and the glory forever. Amen!

ACKNOWLEDGMENTS

To God, for everything.

To Cookie(Mama), for her unwavering support.

To Momoa, my solid backbone (Grandmother).

To Big Mama, for always speaking her mind.

To Rosalind Smith Williams, who inspired me to go out and do it.

To Kenitha Smalls (K. K.), for being my "okay, we've got this" team all by herself. The one who did the real work when I didn't have a clue. What you see in this book is her doing. God will always send you someone at the right time, and this young lady, a fellow church member, was truly sent by God.

And to my readers, you are included because writing this book came from wanting to tell someone that these trials and tribulations do happen, but they are not the *end*.

On March 29, 2024, Baby Genius left, on her journey to the land of forevermore. She will see Cookie, Momoa, Big Mama, and the whole crew with the upmost love and, yes, a broken heart too. I sign off for now because you're just a breath away, so I don't have to say goodbye.

Sweet dreams. The door is unlocked for you! In remembrance of Dana Danelle Henderson (1977–2024).

ABOUT THE AUTHOR

Shara is from Shreveport, Louisiana. She now resides in Jacksonville, Florida. Married and the mother of three adult children, she loves shopping with a passion, traveling, watching horror movies, and listening to jazz music. Her travels taught her about diversity in its truest form, a good lesson to learn and live daily. People and prayer are always foremost in her thoughts.